CAMBRIDGE LIBRARY COLLECTION

Books of enduring scholarly value

Education

This series focuses on educational theory and practice, particularly in the context of eighteenth- and nineteenth-century Europe and its colonies, and America. During this period, the questions of who should be educated, to what age, to what standard and using what curriculum, were widely debated. The reform of schools and universities, the drive towards improving women's education, and the movement for free (or at least low-cost) schools for the poor were all major concerns both for governments and for society at large. The books selected for reissue in this series discuss key issues of their time, including the 'appropriate' levels of instruction for the children of the working classes, the emergence of adult education movements, and proposals for the higher education of women. They also cover topics that still resonate today, such as the nature of education, the role of universities in the diffusion of knowledge, and the involvement of religious groups in establishing and running schools.

Reflections on the Present Condition of the Female Sex

From a prosperous London Quaker family, the author Priscilla Wakefield (1751–1832) wrote educational books for children, including an introduction to botany (also reissued in this series), and this 1798 work for adults, a fascinating piece of social and feminist history. Wakefield argues for better education for women, and suggests ways for those without the support of a husband or family to earn a living. Her ideas are not radical: she divides women into four social classes, with recommendations on appropriate work for each, and she believes that marriage rather than independence is the best outcome for any woman. Her concern for social norms is illustrated by her belief that field labour and any manufacturing job 'where both sexes are promiscuously assembled' are detrimental to female virtue: there are, however, many occupations which do not destroy 'the peculiar characteristic of their sex', or exceed 'the most exact limits of modesty and decorum'.

T0349864

Cambridge University Press has long been a pioneer in the reissuing of out-of-print titles from its own backlist, producing digital reprints of books that are still sought after by scholars and students but could not be reprinted economically using traditional technology. The Cambridge Library Collection extends this activity to a wider range of books which are still of importance to researchers and professionals, either for the source material they contain, or as landmarks in the history of their academic discipline.

Drawing from the world-renowned collections in the Cambridge University Library and other partner libraries, and guided by the advice of experts in each subject area, Cambridge University Press is using state-of-the-art scanning machines in its own Printing House to capture the content of each book selected for inclusion. The files are processed to give a consistently clear, crisp image, and the books finished to the high quality standard for which the Press is recognised around the world. The latest print-on-demand technology ensures that the books will remain available indefinitely, and that orders for single or multiple copies can quickly be supplied.

The Cambridge Library Collection brings back to life books of enduring scholarly value (including out-of-copyright works originally issued by other publishers) across a wide range of disciplines in the humanities and social sciences and in science and technology.

Reflections on the Present Condition of the Female Sex

With Suggestions for its Improvement

PRISCILLA WAKEFIELD

CAMBRIDGE
UNIVERSITY PRESS

CAMBRIDGE
UNIVERSITY PRESS

University Printing House, Cambridge, CB2 8BS, United Kingdom

Cambridge University Press is part of the University of Cambridge.

It furthers the University's mission by disseminating knowledge in the pursuit of
education, learning and research at the highest international levels of excellence.

www.cambridge.org
Information on this title: www.cambridge.org/9781108084710

© in this compilation Cambridge University Press 2015

This edition first published 1798
This digitally printed version 2015

ISBN 978-1-108-08471-0 Paperback

This book reproduces the text of the original edition. The content and language reflect
the beliefs, practices and terminology of their time, and have not been updated.

Cambridge University Press wishes to make clear that the book, unless originally published
by Cambridge, is not being republished by, in association or collaboration with,
or with the endorsement or approval of, the original publisher or its successors in title.

REFLECTIONS

ON THE PRESENT CONDITION OF THE

FEMALE SEX.

REFLECTIONS

ON THE PRESENT CONDITION OF THE

FEMALE SEX;

WITH

SUGGESTIONS FOR ITS IMPROVEMENT.

BY

PRISCILLA WAKEFIELD.

LONDON:

Printed for J. Johnson, in St. Paul's Church-yard ;
and Darton and Harvey, in Gracechurch Street.

1798.

CONTENTS.

CONTENTS.

CONTENTS.

CONTENTS.

REFLECTIONS

FEMALE SEX.

CHAPTER I.

Introductory observations, shewing the claim which Society has on Women to employ their time usefully; pointing out the characteristic perfection of the mental qualifications of both Sexes, and the necessity which there is for the talents of Women being directed towards procuring an independent support; with an attempt to mark the line which bounds their exertions.

IT is asserted by Doctor Adam Smith, that every individual is a burthen upon the society to which he belongs, who does not contribute his share of productive labour for the good of the whole. The Doctor,

B   when

when he lays down this principle,
speaks in general terms of man, as a
being capable of forming a social
compact for mutual defence, and
the advantage of the community at
large. He does not absolutely spe-
cify, that both sexes, in order to
render themselves beneficial members of society, are equally required
to comply with these terms; but since
the female sex is included in the idea
of the species, and as women possess
the same qualities as men, though
perhaps in a different degree, their sex
cannot free them from the claim of the
public for their proportion of useful-
ness. That the major part of the sex,
especially of those among the higher
orders, neglect to fulfil this important obligation, is a fact that must be
admitted, and points out the propriety

priety of an enquiry into the caufes of their deficiency.

The indolent indulgence and trifling purfuits in which thofe who are diftinguifhed by the appellation of gentlewomen, often pafs their lives, may be attributed, with greater probability, to a contracted education, cuftom, falfe pride, and idolizing adulation, than to any defect in their intellectual capacities. The conteft for equality in the mental capacity of the fexes, has been maintained, on each fide of the queftion, with ingenuity; but as a judgment only can be formed from facts, as they arife in the prefent ftate of things, if the experiments have been fairly tried, the rare inftances of extraordinary talents, which have been brought forward to fupport the fyftem of equa-

lity,

lity, muſt yield to the irreſiſtible influence of corporeal powers. Which
leads to a concluſion, that the intellectual faculties of each ſex, are
wiſely adapted to their appropriate
purpoſes, and that, laying aſide the
invidious terms of ſuperiority and
inferiority, the perfection of mind in
man and in woman, conſiſts in a
power to maintain the diſtinguiſhing
characteriſtics of excellence in each.
But this conceſſion by no means
proves, that even in this enlightened
age and country, the talents of women have ever been generally exerted to the utmoſt extent of their
capacity, or that they have been
turned towards the moſt uſeful objects ; neither does it imply, that the
cultivation they receive, is adequate
to bring into action the full ſtrength
of

of thofe powers, which have been beftowed on them by nature. The intellectual faculties of the female mind have too long been confined by narrow and ill-directed modes of education, and thus have been con cealed, not only from others, but from themfelves, the energies of which they are capable. The exigence of circumftances in private life has called forth numberlefs examples of female prudence, magnanimity and fortitude, which demonftrated no lefs a clearnefs of conception, than a warmth of feeling, reflecting equal honour upon the heads, and upon the hearts of the fex. Neither has hif-tory been filent in recording me-morable inftances of female capacity, in all the various branches of human excellence.

B 3   Thefe

Thefe united teftimonies are furely fufficient to juftify an opinion, that the imperfect contributions to the mafs of public activity have not arifen from a want of ability to be ufeful, but from fome defect of another kind, which it is neceffary to difcover, that a remedy may be found, and applied to the evil.

In civilized nations it has ever been the misfortune of the fex to be too highly elevated, or too deeply depreffed; now raifed above the condition of mortals, upon the fcore of their perfonal attractions; and now debafed below that of reafonable creatures, with refpect to their intellectual endowments. The refult of this improper treatment has been a neglect of the mental powers, which women really poffefs, but know not

how

how to exercise; and they have been contented to barter the dignity of reason, for the imaginary privilege of an empire, of the existence of which they can entertain no reasonable hope beyond the duration of youth and beauty.

Of the few who have raised themselves to pre-eminence by daring to stray beyond the accustomed path, the envy of their own sex, and the jealousy or contempt of the other, have too often been the attendants; a fate which doubtless has deterred others from attempting to follow them, or emulate, even in an inferior degree, the distinction they have attained.

But notwithstanding these disadvantages, and others of less perceptible influence, the diffusion of christ-

tianity,

tianity, and the progreſs of civilization, have raiſed the importance of
the female charaĉter; and it has
become a branch of philoſophy, not
a little intereſting, to aſcertain the
offices which the different ranks
of women are required to fulfil.
Their rights and their duties have
lately occupied the pens of writers
of eminence; the employments which
may properly exerciſe their faculties,
and fill up their time in a uſeful
manner, without encroaching upon
thoſe profeſſions, which are appropriate to men, remain to be defined.
There are many branches of ſcience,
as well as uſeful occupations, in
which women may employ their time
and their talents, beneficially to
themſelves and to the community,
without deſtroying the peculiar cha-
racteriſtic

racteriftic of their fex, or exceeding
the moft exact limits of modefty and
decorum. Whatever obliges them
to mix in the public haunts of men,
or places the young in too familiar a
fituation with the other fex; whatever is obnoxious to the delicacy and
referve of the female character, or
deftructive, in the fmalleft degree, to
the ftricteft moral purity, is inadmif-
fible. The fphere of feminine action is contracted by numberlefs difficulties, that are no impediments to
mafculine exertions. Domeftic pri-
vacy is the only fure afylum for the
juvenile part of the fex; nor can the
grave matron ftep far beyond that
boundary with propriety. Unfitted,
by their relative fituation in fociety,
for many honourable and lucrative
employments, thofe only are fuitable
for

for them, which can be purfued without endangering their virtue, or cor-
rupting their manners.

But, under thefe reftrictions, there
may be found a multitude of objects
adapted to the ufeful exertions of female talents, which it will be the
principal defign of thefe Reflections
to point out, after making fome
remarks upon the prefent ftate of
female education, and fuggefting
fome improvements towards its reformation.

And here the author may perhaps
be allowed to exprefs her hope, that
among the numbers of the female
world, who appear to be fatisfied
with inferiority, many require only
to be awakened to a true fenfe of
their own real confequence, to be
induced to fupport it by a rational

im-

improvement of thofe hours, which
they have hitherto wafted in the moft
frivolous occupations. The promotion of fo ufeful a defign, is the
only apology for intruding her opinions upon the fubject; and it will be
efteemed her higheft recompence,
fhould her obfervations contribute to
its accomplifhment.

CHAPTER II.

From the connexion between the Mind and the Body, is deduced the neceſſity of a more hardy mode of rearing Female Children.—The cauſe of an incapacity for ſuckling named, and the miſchiefs attending the practice of hired Nurſes to the Mother, the Child and the Nurſe, deſcribed, with a recommendation of more air and exerciſe being allowed to Girls. —Remarks on riſing, and the propriety of temperance in the rearing of Children enforced.

IT is an opinion, pretty well eſtabliſhed, that the connexion between the mind and the body is of ſo cloſe and reciprocal a nature, that the health of the one materially depends upon the vigorous condition of the other. Though the laws which govern this union lie beyond the reach

of

of human inveftigation, a practical leffon is deducible from the obfer-vation : We are inftructed by it to fortify the body, in order to invigo-rate the powers of the mind. It would be difficult to give a fufficient reafon, why the advantages of the moft probable mode of improving the natural qualities of the one and of the other, are not permitted to be extended with an equal hand to both fexes. The moft obvious folution of this ænigma, is parental folicitude for the prefervation of female beauty; endeavours are ufed to render our fons active, vigorous, and enter-prizing; but the principal care in forming the early habits of our daugh-ters, is the confideration of the ef-fects of thofe habits upon their per-fonal character. Strength, agility, and health,

health, are objects of primary importance, and fhould be equally promoted in the education of girls, as in
that of boys. No apprehenfions need
be entertained of women becoming
too robuft ; their natural inferiority
in ftrength, and the indifpofitions incident to child-bearing, will too often
fecure the feminine delicacy of their
perfons and conftitutions, and prevent them from acquiring more vigour than is requifite to the performance of the active duties of the
mother and the miftrefs of a family.

The Spartans, whofe political inftitutions are ftill celebrated, for
being admirably adapted to produce
a healthy and brave race of citizens,
were particularly attentive to obferve
the moft probable means of render-

2   ing

ing their women robuft, in order to obtain for the children they fhould bring forth, the inheritance of a good conftitution. The effects arifing from this preparatory care fully cor-refponded with the defign, and afford a convincing proof of its advantage. The mind and difpofition of an infant, as well as the conftitution, are probably much influenced by thofe of the mother, efpecially during preg-nancy, a period in which, for that reafon, tumultuous pleafures, violent paffions, and an irregular life, fhould be refolutely avoided. The manners of our women of fafhion, are but ill calculated to prevent the de-generacy of the fpecies; an object of great importance to the public welfare: crowded rooms, late hours, luxurious tables, and flothful inacti-vity,

vity, muſt contribute to the production of a puny offspring, inadequate
to the noble energies of patriotiſm
and virtue.

The ſame cauſes, combined with
the injudicious mode in which they
have been brought up, deprive the
greater part of females in high life,
of the capacity of diſcharging the
firſt maternal office, from which no
rank, however elevated, can exempt
them. The evils conſequent upon
this defect, are of ſufficient magnitude to awaken the moſt ſtrenuous
endeavours to prevent it. That
which ſtrikes the imagination with
the moſt forcible impreſſion, is the
deſtruction, or at leaſt the diminution
of that ſympathy between the mother
and the child, for the promotion of
which, nature has, in a thouſand ways,

fo

fo wifely provided; but others,
equally pernicious and more extenfive, are the frequent attendants of an
inability to perform this facred tafk,
or a voluntary neglect of it. The
helplefs infant is not only banifhed
from the arms of its mother, but is
configned to the care of a fubftitute,
who is tempted, by the expectation of
large gains, to abandon her hufband
and her family, to turn a deaf ear to
the piteous cries of her own offspring,
for that nourifhment, which fhe be-
ftows upon a ftranger. Too frequently the life of this deferted babe
is facrificed ; the hufband is rendered
profligate; and the woman herfelf fo
much corrupted by her new mode
of living, as to be unfitted to return
to her humble ftation.

The effeminate mode of educating

young

young ladies at prefent in vogue, is the fource from whence this defect in the rearing of children in the higher ranks of life originates; an imperfection to which they are almoft exclufively fubject, for there is a very fmall proportion of the labouring poor, who are unable to fuckle their children; whereas a judicious writer afferts, that the converfe of this propofition is true, with refpect to the girls brought up at boarding-fchools, which he attributes chiefly to confinement and want of exercife. The cuftom of many fleeping in the fame chamber may alfo be added, as a probable caufe of general unhealthinefs, as well as of indelicacy and indecorum. The many familiar treatifes which have been written of late years for the ufe of mothers, by perfons

fons eminent for medical abilities, have introduced a far more rational management of children during their infant ftate than formerly, and exploded abfurdities in their food and clothing, which were not deftructive of health and enjoyment only, but alfo of the growth and fymmetry of their limbs.

The fyftem of improvement has been principally confined to the period of infancy; lefs attention feems to have been beftowed upon invigorating the conftitution of girls, as they advance towards maturity; but it is not fufficient to lay a good foundation, fome attention fhould furely be paid to the fuperftructure. The free ufe of air and exercife is the common gift of Heaven, from which none fhould be debarred from

motives

motives of fmall importance; but
how often has an over anxiety for
the delicacy of her complexion, or
the apprehenfion of her becoming a
romp, reftrained a girl from the indulgence of enjoying either, in a
degree fufficient to fecure her from
that feeble, fickly, languid ftate,
which frequently renders her not only
capricious, but helplefs, through the
whole courfe of her life.   There is
no reafon for maintaining any fexual
diftinctions in the bodily exercifes of
children; if it is right to give both
fexes all the corporal advantages,
which nature has formed them to en-
joy, let them both partake of the fame
rational means of obtaining a flow
of health and animal fpirits, to enable
them to perform the functions of
life.   Let girls be no longer confined

to

to fedentary employments in a nur-
fery, or at beft permitted to take a
gentle walk in a garden, as an apology for more vigorous exertions;
whilft their brothers are allowed the
unreftrained enjoyment of their active
powers, regardlefs of foiling their
clothes, or the inconveniences of the
various feafons. The firft occupations of the day fhould be abroad, for
the benefit of inhaling the morning
air; not that their excurfions fhould
be confined to that part of the day
alone, they fhould live out of doors
as much as, poffible, without inter-
fering with the neceffary avocations,
which will fometimes unavoidably
oblige them to remain in the houfe.
Employments fhould be contrived
on purpofe to induce them to pafs a
large portion of their time in the air,

nor

nor fhould they ever be permitted to
fit within long at one time. A mere
walk fcarcely fupplies fufficient exercife to produce a quick circulation,
fomething therefore more active
fhould be adopted: running races,
trundling a hoop, fkipping with a
rope, battledore and fhuttle-cock,
ball, jumping, dumb-bells, fwinging,
and many other amufements of the
like nature, are fuitable for the purpofe, and may, with equal propriety,
be practifed by both fexes, being by
no means incompatible with delicacy
of perfon or manners. Let it never
be forgotten, that true delicacy confifts in purity of fentiment, and is as
much fuperior to its fubftitute, external manners, as is a real gem to
one that is artificial.

Though girls may not be able to
bear

bear the extremes of heat and cold·
fo well as boys, yet, by gradual advances, they may be enured to bear
the tranfitions of the feafons without
much inconvenience; nor ought they,
if healthy, to be fo tender as to be confined to the houfe by the coldeft day
that is felt in our climate. An habitual ufe of the cold bath is conducive
to fortify the habit, and enable it to
refift the changes of the atmofphere;
where that cannot be obtained, a
liberal ufe of cold water fhould be
fubftituted for it, as neceffary for the
combined purpofes of health, and
cleanlinefs of perfon. It is a miftaken notion, that children fhould
wear the fame clothing in winter as
in fummer, with defign to make
them hardy; in this changeable climate, their drefs fhould be regulated

by

by the weather, and warm flannel
petticoats and worsted stockings, may
be confidered as neceffary for maintaining a brisk circulation, and encouraging a willingnefs to play abroad
when the cold is fevere. Warmth,
lightnefs, and convenience, are effential requifites in the drefs of a child;
every reftraint that tends to diftort,
and comprefs any part of the body,
is as injurious to grace and proportion, as to health. Steel collars,
braces, back-boards, and feet-ftocks,
may be carried to a very dangerous
excefs, and caufe that deformity,
which they are intended to prevent.

Length of time is neceffary to
confirm the afcendancy of reafon
over eftablifhed prejudices; our great-
grandmothers would have been a-
larmed for the fafety of an infant,

2   whofe

whofe head had not been confined
with a bridle, its body bound with a
long bandage of flannel, and its hands
pinned down under a napkin, during
at leaſt the firſt ſix months of its life.
Neither could they have reconciled
to their falſe notions of modeſty, the
appearing in public without the en-
cloſure of ſtays, reſembling the ar-
mour of ancient warriors, in their
unwieldy form and texture. Experience has proved the utility of theſe
alterations; inſtances of deformity are
rare among women to what they
were formerly, when tight and ſtiff
ſtays were in general uſe. The ſuperior elegance of the preſent eaſy
mode, will probably ſecure it from
the effects of the verſatile ſpirit of
faſhion, and ſupport it more powerfully, than even its phyſical advantages, great as they are acknowledged

ledged to be. It is defirable that the lower claffes fhould partake of the benefits of this improvement in female apparel, and that leathern bodice and whalebone ftays fhould be indifcriminately banifhed together; for, fo far from thefe unyielding machines affording fupport to the wearer, and affifting her to perform laborious employments with greater eafe, they are a painful impediment to the motions of the body, and prevent the full exertion of her ftrength.

The advantages of early rifing, at every period of life, are fo obvious, that it feems almoft unneceffary to enforce it, as of effential moment in forming the early habits of children ; but a caution may not be ufelefs againft either extreme, of difturbing a child out of its natural fleep, or fuffering it to fall afleep again, when

once

once thoroughly awakened. When
a child is accuſtomed to riſe as ſoon
as it wakes, it will not be difficult to
continue it in that practice. Healthy
children are generally alert and lively
as ſoon as they open their eyes, and
free from that ſluggiſh heavineſs,
to which adults are often ſubject,
either from the groſſneſs, or abun-
dant quantity of their food; or from
a propenſity to the indulgence of
more ſleep than nature requires.

Temperance ſhould be inculcated
as a moral obligation, no leſs than as
a preſervative of health and cheerfulneſs. It conſiſts not only in
ſimplicity of diet, but in a re-
ſtriction as to exceſs in quantity.
Let the food of children be whole-
ſome, nouriſhing, and void of al-
lurements to eat more than is required

quired to fatisfy the appetite. Their
meals fhould be regular, and return
fufficiently often, to prevent long
abftinence, which is injurious to their
growth; but they fhould never be
indulged in the improper cuftom of
eating or drinking between the ftated
times.

Thefe few hints upon the perfonal
management of girls, as far as relates
to the promotion of their health,
appeared to belong to the plan of
the work; but as education is not
its principal object, general obfervations are fufficient for the purpofe;
the fubject having been treated more
at large by much abler pens. It is
only intended to recommend a fyftem of greater energy, as preparja-
tory to a more vigorous cultivation
of the mental faculties.

CHAPTER III.

Remarks on the duties of a married and a single life.—Maternal tuition, when practicable, recommended; with a sketch of the qualifications of a Governess.—Plan suggested for a Female College, and Select Day Schools proposed.—Ranks in society discriminated.—The necessity of Women being educated for the exercise of lucrative employments shewn, and the absurdity of a Woman honourably earning a support, being excluded from Society, exposed.

In the education of females, the same view actuates every rank: an advantageous settlement in marriage is the universal prize, for which parents of all classes enter their daughters upon the lists; and partiality or self complacency assures to every competitor the most flattering prospect of success. To this one point tends

tends the principal part of female inftruction; for the promotion of this defign, their beft years for improvement are facrificed to the attainment of attractive qualities, fhewy fuperficial accomplifhments, polifhed manners, and in one word, the whole fcience of pleafing, which is cultivated with unceafing affiduity, as an object of the moft effential importance.

The end is laudable, and deferving of every effort that can be exerted to fecure it; a happy marriage may be eftimated among the rareft felicities of human life; but it may be doubted, whether the means ufed to accomplifh it are adequate to the purpofe; as the making a firft impreffion, is by no means effectual to determine the preference of a wife man.

man. It is not then fufficient, that
a girl be qualified to excite admiration; her own happinefs, and that of
the man to whom fhe devotes the
remainder of her days, depend upon
her poffeffion of thofe virtues, which
alone can preferve lafting efteem and
confidence.

The offices of a wife are very different from thofe of the mere pa-
geant of a ball-room; and as their
nature is more exalted, the talents
they require are of a more noble
kind: fomething far beyond the elegant trifler is wanted in a companion
for life. A young woman is very ill-
adapted to enter into the moft folemn
of focial contracts, who is not prepared, by her education, to become
the participator of her hufband's cares,
the confoler of his forrows, his fti-
mulator

mulator to every praife-worthy undertaking, his partner in the labours
and viciffitudes of life, the faithful
and œconomical manager of his affairs, the judicious fuperintendant of
his family, the wife and affectionate
mother of his children, the preferver
of his honour, his chief counfellor,
and, to fum up all, the chofen friend
of his bofom. If a modern female
education be not calculated to produce thefe effects, as few furely
will judge it to be, who reflect upon
its tendency, it is incompetent to
that very purpofe, which is confef-
fedly its main object, and muft therefore be deemed imperfect, and require reformation.

Before the defects of the prefent
fyftem are pointed out, let an enquiry
alfo take place, whether it be better
fuited

fuited to qualify women for fuftain-
ing the other characters which they
may be deftined to fulfil. Thofe of
widowhood and a fingle life are the
allotment of many, and to fupport
them with dignity, requires peculiar
force of mind. Adverfity often places
both fexes in fituations wholly unexpected; againft fuch tranfitions,
the voice of wifdom admonifhes each
to be prepared, by early initiation
into general principles fuited to fortify
the mind, to fuftain the unavoidable
ftrokes of fortune with firmnefs, and
to exert the moft prudent means to
obviate their confequences; but the
bias given to the female mind in
the prefent fyftem of education, en-
courages the keeneft fenfibility on the
moft trifling occafions, its chief de-

D   fign

fign being to polifh, rather than to
ftrengthen.

The regulation of the temper, is
of all qualities the moft ufeful to
conduct us fteadily through the vex-
atious circumftances, which attack,
with undiftinguifhing annoyance, the
profperous and the unfortunate ; and
is fupereminently neceffary to women, whofe peculiar office it is, to
fmooth the inconveniences of domeftic life; though as a moral obligation, equally incumbent upon men.
A well governed temper is the fupport of focial enjoyment, and the
bond of conjugal affection ; deficient
in this qualification, a mother is in-
capacitated from prefiding over the
education of her children, and a miftrefs unfitted to govern her fervants.
The felf command recommended,
2   differs

differs widely from that apathy of difpofition, which is the effect of conftitution; in order to enfure refpect and love, it muft poffefs an equability, which can only refult from reflection and habitual culture, Such a fubjection of the angry paffions to reafon and duty, accommodates itfelf to circumftances, and the difpofition of others with whom we are connected; it gives a decided fuperiority in every conteft, and is of ineftimable value to the poffeffor, on every occafion of trial.

The chief fources of caprice and petulance, are weaknefs of underftanding, or early habits of unreftrained indulgence; the firft is a misfortune, but the laft fhould be guarded againft with the ftricteft precaution. A girl fhould be impreffed,

from

from the firſt dawnings of reaſon, that
ſhe lives, not for herſelf only, but to
contribute to the happineſs of others ;
let her be ſometimes told, that in
the probable events of futurity, her
path of duty may lie in ſharing the
cares of her huſband, perhaps in
conſoling him under misfortunes,
and in bearing patiently the inequa-
lities of his temper, ruffled by ad-
verſe accidents ; that ſo far from
ſhewing diſcontent, it will be her
part to ſoften theſe aſperities, by a
ſteady command over her own paſſions, which can only be attained by
continual exercife, opportunities for
which, the minute occurrences of ſo-
cial and domeſtic life will daily preſent. That ſhould her deſtination
be to remain an inhabitant in her father's houſe, cheerfulneſs, good temper,

per, and an obliging refignation of her will to that of others, will be there equally her duty, and her intereft ; that it will belong to her to enliven, to cheer, to amufe the latter moments of her parent's declining age ; that the virtue neceffary for bearing with the infirmities of mind and body, incident to thofe days in which there is no pleafure, is not the momentary effufion of good-humour, but an even principle, too firmly eftablifhed to be difconcerted by trifling incidents; that it is a branch of that charity, which fuffereth long, and is kind, which envieth not, nor vaunteth itfelf, nor is puffed up, neither is it eafily provoked ; that it extends with equal benignity to the noble and the mean, and that it never fhines with more diftinguifhed luftre,

than

than in a conteſt with a rival, over whom it forbids to triumph, even in the moment of victory.

Is it becauſe the vanity of parents and governeſſes induces them to be-ſtow the moſt-aſſiduous pains in the inſtruction of their pupils, in thoſe accompliſhments, which ſtrike the obſerver with an equal degree of ad-miration for the talents of the teacher, as for thoſe of the ſcholar, that the regulation of the temper, and prin-ciples, objects leſs calculated to ex-cite the attention of ſtrangers, are abandoned to the uncertain influence of accidental impreſſions. Or is the culture of the heart ſo much more difficult than that of the head, that few attempt the taſk by any other means, than by dry unimpreſſive lectures, which are forgotten as ſoon

as

as they are paſt, and are totally in-
efficacious to influence the conduct?
The indiſpenſable obligation of forming the morals and diſpoſitions of
our ſcholars, by example, increaſes
the obſtacles to this branch of education, and is a probable cauſe of
the general deficiency in it. Mothers only can be expected to make
the ſacrifices neceſſary for this important work; no other perſon can
feel the ſame intereſt in the event,
nor can any occupation in which
they may be engaged have ſo powerful a claim upon their attention, unleſs it be for the actual ſupport of
the family. It is a very erroneous
miſapplication of time, for a woman
who fills the honourable and re-
ſponſible character of a parent, to
waſte her days in the frivolous em-

ployment

ployment of needle-work, or the executive minutiæ of domeſtic affairs, for which ſubſtitutes of equal ability may be ſo eaſily provided, if ſhe be capable of taking an active part in forming the minds of her children. Surely it would be a more profitable diſpoſal of time and money, to appoint a houſe-keeper to perform theſe concerns of inferior importance, and to diſcharge in perſon the tender and eſſential office of governeſs; at leaſt, as far as reſpects principles, religion, morals, and the cultivation of the heart. But let not any mother preſume to engage in this ſacred and delightful taſk, without firſt enquiring of herſelf, whether ſhe be able to renounce foreign pleaſures, whether ſhe can reſtrain herſelf from the diſſipated indulgence, authoriſed by cuſtom to

thoſe

thofe in affluent circumftances; whether fhe have courage and perfeverance to rife early and watch late, to devote her whole time and undivided attention to this one great objeƈt, and finally, whether fhe can rely upon herfelf, to fet fuch an example of felf-government, as fhall illuftrate her own precepts in the moft forcible manner.

Difficult as thefe qualifications may appear to be of attainment, they need not deter the humble and the diffident, who are fincerely attached to the beft interefts of their off-fpring : earneftnefs in the caufe, and a determination to peıform the part of duty, will overcome barriers that feem infurmountable. Maternal affeƈtion properly direƈted, with fortitude, and application, will capa-

citate

citate for the office, and enable an
affiduous mother to fucceed better,
than any delegate fhe can engage,
whatever may be her pretenfions.
No doubt can be entertained, but
that a fure reward will follow this
facrifice to duty, befides that of the
pleafure of the employment; fhould
even the moft judicious and unre-
mitted endeavours be fruftrated by a
perverfe difpofition, or an unhappy
concurrence of circumftances, a confcioufnefs of having performed the
part affigned by nature, according to
the moft deliberative judgment, will
fupply confolation in the moft afflict-
ing moments of mifconduct and in-
gratitude; when thofe who have neglected the fuperintendance of their
children's education for other purfuits, may reflect upon themfelves
for

for not having done their utmoſt, to prevent ſo great an evil.—This advantage alone, without infiſting upon the greater probability of ſucceſs than of failure, is ſufficient to give a decided preference to the education of girls under the maternal eye.

But after every argument has been urged in favour of domeſtic inſtruction, it muſt be acknowledged, that there are many circumſtances which render the adoption of it improper ; ſuch as want of health, temper, or ability ; avocations that cannot be diſpenſed with ; a huſband's diſapprobation, and various other peculiarities of ſituation which completely exonerate a mother from the undertaking; it is contended only, that where it is practicable, it is always defirable,.and that, in proportion as the

the cuſtom becomes prevalent, female diſſipation will decline. A woman earneſtly occupied in this moſt
intereſting of all engagements, has
no leiſure to court the ſtupid gaze of
caſual admiration : dreſs and public
diverſions of courſe loſe their at-
traction, her treaſure is at home,
and where the treaſure is, there is
high authority for believing that the
heart will be. Some of the unhappy
deviations from conjugal fidelity,
which of late years have ſo often
given employment to the gentlemen
of Doctors Commons, might probably have never diſgraced our courts
of juſtice, nor thrown a public odium
upon the ſex, had the wretched de-
linquents fulfilled the tender duties
of the maternal character. Were it
poſſible to trace the majority of
theſe

thefe miferable inftances of depra-
vity to their fource, it is reafonable
to believe, that the firft falfe ftep
would be found to proceed from the
want of energetic employment, an
indolent vacuity of mind, which produced a wearifome reftlefsnefs, and
led to diffipation as a relief. How
dangerous fuch refources are, has
alas too frequently been manifeft!
It is fcarcely a poffible fuppofition,
that the boldeft feducer, however
confident in the impofing influence
of his arts to betray, fhould dare to
whifper his unhallowed love in the
ear of her, whom he faw devoted to
the duties of the conjugal ftate, and
daily employed in the education of
her children; whofe time was unceaf-
ingly filled up with a fucceffion of
well-chofen objeds : a flight acquaintance

quaintance would convince him, that
fhe was a hopelers purfuit, and that
there was no chance of fuccefs with
one, whofe mind was fo virtuoufly
pre-occupied. Let then interefting
employment, fuch as deferve the
name of bufinefs, be purfued as a
talifman, to preferve thofe women
who are virtuous, from becoming
victims to the delufions of vice; and
if fuch be the efficacy of occupation,
mothers of all degrees cannot too
earneftly habituate their daughters to
daily application to fome object of
real utility.

When parents are compelled to
refign their tender charge to the care
of others, what cautions are neceffary
in the choice of the perfons to whom
they are entrufted! After having
expatiated upon the requifites of a
maternal

maternal preceptor, it is almoſt
needleſs to remark, that few of the
candidates for the important office of
educating youth, are fitted for it;
nay, very few have even an idea of
the ſevere ſacrifices which the undertaking requires, if it is properly
performed. How many mothers
ſhrink from the taſk, unable to ſub-
mit to the fatigue, and confer it upon
ſtrangers, whoſe principal recommendation too frequently is their
poverty. The miſtreſs of the ſe-
minary, is perhaps by birth a gen-
tlewoman, reduced by adverſity to
feek a ſupport from ſuch an eſtabliſhment; her mind may have been
enlarged by liberal inſtruction, and
her heart raiſed above mere ſordid
views; but if her ſcholars be numerous, ſhe is obliged, from the
preſſure

preſſure of her avocations, to make
a ſecond transfer of her pupils to the
tuition and ſociety of her teachers;
a claſs of women, generally ſpeaking,
for there are doubtleſs many reſpec-
table exceptions, who are both igno-
rant and unprincipled; a ſmattering
of the French language, and ſkill
in the ornamental works which are
in vogue, conſtitute their chief knowledge. The misfortunes of individuals, occaſioned by the revolution
of France, has probably furniſhed a
ſupply of theſe ſubordinate inſtruc-
tors, better qualified for their office;
but antecedent to the period above-
mentioned, many natives of that
country, who had loſt their characters at home, came here, and found
employment as teachers in our
boarding-ſchools. Thoſe who pre-
ſide

fide over inftitutions for the education
of children, whether male or female,
can never be too confcientioufly
fcrupulous in felecting fuch affiftants
only, whofe moral characters will
bear the ftricteft inveftigation. It is
to be feared that a preference is often
given to thofe, who will engage for
the loweft falary, without fearching
very clofely into any of their qualifications, beyond thofe of a fuperficial
knowledge of the common accomplifhments. Principles, exemplary
conduct, and experience in their
profeffions, are overlooked as things
too rare to be found.

The difficulty of meeting with perfons properly qualified to be the
preceptors and guides of the uncor-
rupted minds of youth, is allowed to
be great, and fuggefts the advantages

E   which

which might arise, from the establishment of institutions for the express purpose of educating young women, of small expectations, for the office. These institutions should be sufficiently endowed, to provide masters in every useful science, and to furnish a well-chosen library, consisting of the most approved authors, with globes, and other suitable apparatus for instruction, and after a certain number of years, women only should be nominated to the charge of instruction. The effect of such seminaries would be a constant succession of female teachers properly prepared for their destination, not only by a regular course of study, but also by a thorough initiation into the philosophical principles of education, founded upon the opinions

of

of the moſt eminent writers upon the
ſubjeƈt. Another beneficial conſequence would be, the affording a re-
ſpeƈtable ſubſiſtence to great numbers
of young women, who are reduced
to miſery through want of employment, by enabling them to teach
thoſe ſciences, which are excluſively taught by maſters, an evil
that calls loudly for redreſs. Surely
it can never be denied, that the in-
ſtruƈtion of girls in every department of knowledge or art, is a fair
field for the exertion of female talents. Is it compatible with propriety or decency, that the perſons of
girls advancing towards maturity,
ſhould be expoſed to the wanton eye
of a dancing-maſter? Are not the
faſcinating tones of muſic as dangerous as the graces of dancing, in ex-

E 2   citing

citing the tender emotions? Women only, therefore, fhould be permitted to inftruct the fex in thefe feductive arts. It ought to be their privilege to do fo in every other. Nature has impofed no invincible barrier to their acquifition and communication of languages, arithmetic, writing, drawing, geography, or any fcience which is proper for girls to learn. Some efforts feem already to have been made for promoting the fubftitution of female teachers inftead of mafters. In many fchools of eminence mufic is taught by female profeffors; but the entire exclufion of mafters from girls boarding-fchools can never be effected, until a fufficient number of women are qualified to fupply their places, and the plan is patronized by parents and guardians. Were a due

con-

confideration of this fubject to take
place in the minds of the public, the
advantages are fo many, and fo obvious, that a decided preference
would certainly be given to all female
inftructors, when equally qualified by
a profound knowledge of the peculiar department of fcience they pro-
fefs to teach, as thofe male profeffors
who have fo long fupplanted them in
occupations to which they alone have
a reafonable claim.

Whilft we remain without a provifion for a more regular courfe of
preparation for the refpective offices
of governefs and teacher, not only
in the various branches of inftruction,
but likewife in the particular knowledge which is effential to their
profeffion, by which is meant, a philofophical knowledge, founded upon

E 3   prin-

principle, of cultivating the heart,
and forming the future character;
by correcting the depraved propen-
sities of the former, and substituting
in their places fixed habits of virtue;
a confiderable improvement upon
the present plan might be effected,
by the appropriation of fchools to
the different claffes of fociety. At
prefent there is fcarcely any difcrimination between the daughters of
noblemen and thofe of tradefmen,
they are both educated upon nearly
the fame fyftem, without any reference to their future deftination in
life. The opulent can afford to pay
fuch a ftipend with their children,
as may enable the proprietor to re-
ftrict her number, to as many only
as fhe can inftruct herfelf; which
would give her an opportunity of
ftudy-

ftudying the difpofition and natural
character of each of her pupils, and
capacitate her to apply remedies
adapted to reform their peculiar defects. A fchool upon fuch a foundation, under the direction of a judicious perfon, would poffefs the advantages of private education, combined with thofe of focial inftruction,
unalloyed by the evils which are unavoidable in large feminaries. As
the expence of a very confined number, fupported in a genteel ftyle, and
recompenfing the governefs liberally
for the whole of her time and attention, would exceed the ability of moderate circumftances; felect day-
fchools, preferved fo by terms proportioned to the clafs for the ufe of
which they are defigned, fhould be
generally inftituted for the accommodation

modation of thofe parents, whom prudence reftrains from fending their children to boarding-fchools of the above defcription. Day-fchools, if preferved from an improper mixture of children, are preferable in many refpects to boarding-fchools, as they afford opportunities for maternal in-ftruction, in the intervals between the hours of attendance, to thofe parents who are prevented from taking the entire charge of the education of their daughters, either by domeftic avocations, or the rearing a fucceffion of younger children, and are obliged to have recourfe to a fchool for their learning, yet can fpare a little leifure, without detriment to their families, to the improvement of their minds in thofe things, which cannot be fo effectually impreffed by general pre-

cepts

cepts delivered to numbers, as in the retirement of familiar converſation. Opportunities of conveying much uſeful knowledge, which can only be acquired in a private family, may frequently occur to a mother, watchful of every occaſion of ſuggeſting inſtruction; domeſtic œconomy, tender offices to the ſick, the management of infants, and other occupations of a ſimilar nature, may furniſh amuſement as well as inſtruction to girls above ten years of age, during their hours of recreation, both from the novelty of the employments, and the conſequence annexed to the exerciſe of them.

There cannot be a more miſtaken tendernefs than to give an education to our children diſproportioned to the rank they are likely to fill in ſociety.

ciety. Tradefmen and mechanics
are fond of bringing up their daughters in what they term a genteel
manner; that is, fending them, at
a very inconvenient expence, perhaps as half-boarders, to an elegant
boarding-fchool, where they prefently imbibe a defire of emulating
their fuperiors in drefs, fhewy qualifications and fafhionable folly. They
fhould not only be prohibited from
learning the ornamental arts, fuch as
mufic, dancing, drawing, foreign
languages, and coftly works of tafte,
(unlefs they are brought up for
teachers) but they fhould never be
placed at a fchool where thofe arts
are taught; for it is a natural propenfity of the human mind, to prefer
that which is beautiful and pleafant,
to thofe things which though ufeful
are

are unadorned. Refpectable fchools, not aiming at gentility, as it is ufually termed, fhould therefore be eftablifhed for the exprefs purpofe of educating young women of this clafs, where they might acquire whatever knowledge is conducive to render them ufeful in their ftation, without having their fimplicity corrupted by an intercourfe with thofe, who have a reafonable title to the indulgences of affluence, and the acquifition of liberal accomplifhments. The defign of early inftruction is to qualify the pupil to perform that part, which it is probable will be her future allotment; confequently whatever defeats this purpofe is abfurd; a refined education is therefore extremely improper for thofe, whofe humble views confine them to the employments of

an

an inferior ſtation. Falſe notions of enjoyment, and a dangerous taſte for elegance, acquired at boarding-ſchool, have been the unhappy means of caſting many women ſo ſituated into the abyſs of proſtitution. Too proud for the lowly occupations of their parents, and filled with the ambition of obtaining a ſettlement above that of their equals, they imagine that they have only to diſplay the charms of youth and beauty, adorned by·a modiſh ſtyle of dreſs, to enſure an eſtabliſhment that will be anſwerable to their wiſhes; but inſtead of promoting a laſting advantage, this ridiculous conduct frequently expoſes them to the obſervation of the vicious, amongſt thoſe who rank as their ſuperiors of the oppoſite ſex, who beſet them with tempta-

temptations, irrefiftible to minds de-
void of fixed principles of right and
wrong, and whofe peculiar errors
affift to betray them into the fnare
that is laid for them.

The injudicious practice of bringing up girls above their expectations,
originates in a common opinion, that
a good education is more valuable
than a dowry; the fentiment is a juft
one, the error confifts in a mifap-
prehenfion of what conftitutes a
good education: No fyftem of inftruction can properly be denominated good, which is not appropriate to thofe who receive it: Of what
ufe would it be to a feaman to learn
the theory of agriculture ? To him
it would be only a fpeculative knowledge, which he could not apply in
the exercife of his profeffion; neither
would

would many parts of nautical ſkill, which are indiſpenſable to an admiral, whoſe office is to command a fleet, be of ſervice to a ſailor before the maſt, whoſe buſineſs is confined to the ſervile departments of a ſeafaring life. A ſimilar appropriation of qualifications to fortune and expectations, is neceſſary likewiſe amongſt women, for it cannot be ſuppoſed that a butcher's wife will ſerve her huſband's cuſtomers, or a moderate farmer's daughter manage the dairy or the poultry-yard with more adroitneſs, for knowing how to walk a minuet, or to play upon the harpſichord. In order therefore to fit every one for their ſtation, ſchools ſhould be eſtabliſhed adapted to the different deſcriptions of children.

Society

Society may be refolved into four
claffes or degrees; the firft compre-
hends the nobility, and all thofe who,
either by the influence of high offices,
or extenfive hereditary poffeffions,
rival them in power; the fecond con-
tains thofe, who by the application
of their talents to learning, commerce, manufactures or agriculture,
procure a refpectable fubfiftence ap-
proaching to opulence; to the third
may be referred thofe, whofe honeft
and ufeful induftry raifes them above
want, without procuring for them
the means of fplendid or luxurious
gratification: The fourth is compofed of the labouring poor: The
rank of women being determined by
the accident of their birth, or their
connections in marriage, a corre-
fpondent arrangement is, with equal
pro-

propriety, applicable to them, as to the other fex.

An inquiry into the objects of attainment, employments, and pursuits of the different claffes of the one fex, will throw light upon thofe that ought to occupy the corresponding ranks of the other.

Noblemen, and gentlemen of independent property, receive a courfe of inftruction adapted to prepare them for filling up the higheft offices in the different departments of the ftate, confiftently with their own dignity, and the fervice of their country; or to maintain the inviolability of our valuable conftitution, as diftinguifhed ornaments in the fenate, or at the bar.——The learned profeffions, or the lucrative and refpectable avocations of commercial life, are

4   fources

fources of honour and wealth to
the inferior gentry and merchants.
Farmers, tradefmen and artificers,
befides the general acquifition of the
fimpler branches of learning, attain
the knowledge of fome peculiar art,
or branch of commerce, by which
they are enabled to gain a competent
fupport.

The neceffity of directing the attention of females to fome certain
occupation is not fo apparent, becaufe cuftom has rendered them
dependant upon their fathers and
hufbands for fupport; but as fome of
every clafs experience the lofs of
thofe relations, without inheriting an
adequate refource, there would be
great propriety in preparing each of
them, by an education of energy and
ufeful attainments, to meet fuch dif-

F   afters,

afters, and to be able, under such circumstances, to procure an independence for themselves. There is
scarcely a more helpless object in the
wide circle of misery which the vi-
cissitudes of civilized society display,
than a woman genteelly educated,
whether single or married, who is
deprived, by any unfortunate accident, of the protection and support
of male relations; unaccustomed to
struggle with difficulty, unacquainted
with any resource to supply an independent maintenance, she is reduced
to the depths of wretchedness, and
not unfrequently, if she be young and
handsome, is driven by despair to
those paths which lead to infamy.
Is it not time to find a remedy for
such evils, when the contention of
nations has produced the most af-
fecting

fecting tranfitions in private life, and
transferred the affluent and the noble
to the humiliating extremes of want
and obfcurity ? When our ftreets
teem with multitudes of unhappy
women, many of whom might have
been refcued from their prefent degradation, or who would perhaps
never have fallen into it, had they
been inftructed in the exercife of
fome art or profeffion, which would
have enabled them to procure for
themfelves a refpectable fupport by
their own induftry.

This reafonable precaution againft
the accidents of life is refifted by
prejudice, which rifes like an infurmountable barrier againft a woman,
of any degree above the vulgar, em-
ploying her time and her abilities,
towards the maintenance of herfelf

and

and her family : degradation of rank immediately follows the virtuous attempt, as it did formerly, among the younger branches of the noble families in France. But the nature of truth is immutable, however it may be obſcured by error: that which is a moral excellence in one rational being, deſerves the ſame eſtimation in another; therefore, if it be really honourable in a man, to exert the utmoſt of his abilities, whether mental or corporal, in the acquiſition of a competent ſupport for himſelf, and for thoſe who have a natural claim upon his protection; it muſt be equally ſo in a woman, nay, perhaps ſtill more incumbent, as in many caſes, there is nothing ſo inimical to the preſervation of her virtue as a ſtate of poverty, which

leaves

leaves her dependant upon the ge-
nerofity of others, to fupply thofe
accommodations, which ufe has rendered neceffary to her comfort.

There appears then no moral impediment to prevent women from
the application of their talents to purpofes of utility; on the contrary, an
improvement in public manners muſt
infallibly refult from it; as their influence over the other fex is univerfally acknowledged, it may be boldly
afferted, that a converfion of their
time from trifling and unproductive
employments, to thofe that are both
ufeful and profitable, would operate
as a check upon luxury, diffipation,
and prodigality, and retard the progrefs of that general diffolutenefs,
the offspring of idlenefs, which is

depre-

deprecated by all political writers, as the fure forerunner of national decay.

Some alteration in the general turn of thinking among young women, muft take place before they can be perfuaded to render themfelves capable of thefe ufeful exertions; and that can be produced only by the early impreffions they imbibe; the manner in which they are received in fociety, after fuch application; and their finding no impediment arife from it to their fettlement in marriage. It cannot be expected that young females will of choice apply themfelves to ferious ftudies, or be willing to become induftrious members of the community, whilft they are impreffed from infancy with a notion, that they are born only to

4   create

create admiration, and that they are
excluded from the neceffity of any
regular occupation, beyond that of
domeftic fuperintendance, or what
conduces to the acquifition of elegant accomplifhments. The correction of thefe errors depends upon
the difcretion of thofe, whofe duty
it is to form their opinions upon juft
principles. But their reception in
fociety refts not upon the propriety
of their fentiments, or the prudence
of their conduct, in this refpect; it
can only be affured to them by perfons of rank and confequence, whofe
countenance will be fufficient gradually to undermine the unreafonable prepoffeffion againft the exercife
of female induftry. Can it be accounted for on any other ground
than that of prejudice, in a country

like

like England, where commerce forms
one of the principal finews of national
ftrength, where the character of the
merchant is honourable, and no ob-
ftacle to a favourable reception in
the higheft circles, that degradation
fhould attend the female who en-
gages in the concerns of commerce,
and that fhe whofe good fenfe and
refolution enable her to fupport herfelf, is banifhed from that line of
company, of which fhe had perhaps
previoufly formed a diftinguifhed
ornament? One of the effects of
this ill-directed pride, is to deter
young men of liberal profpects, from
demeaning themfelves, as it is erro-
neoufly termed, by marrying a girl
who has been trained up to any profitable employment. How much
more reafonable would it be to give
them

them a preference on account of this
mark of their fuperior judgment,
which may fairly be eftimated as
an earneft of their becoming ufeful
helpmates through the uncertain contingency of future events.

Were but thefe three barriers re-
moved, of falfe notions, exclufion
from fociety, or diminifhing the
chance of an advantageous marriage;
the example of a few might influence
others, and extend like a drop of oil
fpread upon the furface of the water.
But where are the parents, who have
fufficient independence of mind to
encourage their daughters to lead
the way, and to prepare them, by an
improved plan of education, to fucceed in it? To lay afide the fetters
of prejudice, and adopt a practice
contrary to eftablifhed cuftoms, requires

quires a cool unbiaffed judgment, and unfhaken refolution to comply with its dictates. The utility of the ob-ject would apologize for the innova-tion, and the difficulty of the at-tempt but enhances its merit. The word reform, has become the fignal of a party, and the fear of change may render fome averfe from the very idea of introducing an alteration in female manners : But let fuch be informed, that it is not a novelty that is pro-pofed; the Dutch adopted it in part a century ago, as we are told by Sir Jofiah Child, in his difcourfe con-cerning trade, wherein he remarks that the education of the Dutch wo-men prepared them to receive in-ftruction from their hufbands, in the different fpecies of commerce in which they were engaged : He re-
commends

commends the imitation of this example to the Englifh, as one of the
means that promoted the riches and
profperity of Holland; and contri-
buted in no fmall degree to the happinefs of individuals: And as he
does not ftate that any inconvenience
arofe from this practice, it is
candid to fuppofe that this ufeful
knowledge had no ill effect upon the
Dutch women, to render them independent of their hufbands, or lefs
fubmiffive to their authority, than
the wives of modern times.

The firft ftep to be purfued towards this defirable improvement, is
the adoption of a more energetic
mode of education. Inftruction has
been beftowed upon girls with a
much greater liberality of late years
than formerly; and it will fcarcely
be

be controverted, that the beneficial
effects of it are apparent, in the improved state of female knowledge
and conduct. But they are still
taught, what they learn, too super-
ficially, and the more solid acquirements are too often neglected. Mufic, dancing, drefs, and works of
fancy, engrofs a larger fhare of time
and attention than is their due : they
fhould be regarded as amufements,
rather than as occupations, and be
reftrained within a proper fubordi-
nation to thofe purfuits, which are
fuperior in their nature and confequence. The importance of promoting health and vigour of conftitution, has been already fuggefted as
a fuitable foundation for the attainment of ftrength of mind; with which
may properly be combined, whatever

ever is conducive to perſonal beauty
or graceful deportment; for it is not
aſſerted, that external appearance is
unworthy of all regard, it certainly
claims a due attention; but it is ad-
viſable to temper that care with
every poſſible precaution againſt ex-
citing the emotions of ſelf-compla-
cency and perſonal vanity, the moſt
dangerous of all qualities in a female
mind, as they are the ſource of the
moſt common errors in female conduct. One injurious conſequence of
a vain mind, is an extravagant taſte
for dreſs, and exhibiting the perſon
in public places; a diſpoſition ſubver-
ſive of domeſtic happineſs, and that
ſobriety of character, which, in youth,
is the preſage of every thing uſeful
and honourable.

CHAPTER IV.

*On the Duties, Studies, and Amusements of Wo-
men of the first class in Society.*

AMIDST the numerous resources
of talent and genius, those who have
been unhappily accustomed to habits
of indolence, and a succession of
light amusements, will languish, incapable of relishing the enjoyment
they produce, or cultivating them
with success.

Man is a being endued with certain powers, which, if suffered to lie
dormant, become torpid and useless;
the energy of action alone can pre-
serve them in perfection; and one of
these, which especially requires exercise to maintain it in vigour, is the
capacity of application. The habit

of

of using this faculty, which may be
confidered as the inftrument of acquiring every branch of human
knowledge, can feldom, without
great refolution and exertion, be
gained after childhood is paffed; how
neceffary then is it to enure the infant
mind to the practice of daily and vigorous application! Labour is the
price of knowledge, as indeed it is
of every other valuable poffeffion
which is placed within our attainment; neither health, nor the activity
of the intellectual powers, nor even
pleafure itfelf can be enjoyed unlefs
purchafed by exertion. If fuch be
the conftitution of our nature, let the
ambition of women be directed to
affert their claim to the characteriftic
mark of rational beings, and to rife
above the enervating habits of indolent

lent indulgence; let them ftrengthen
their bodies by exercife, and their
minds by cultivation, till they acquire
the full ufe of thofe powers, which
have been beftowed upon them by a
beneficent Creator, for the purpofe
of qualifying them to perform that
part in the world, to which his pro-
vidence has appointed them.

The different orders or conditions
of mankind require the performance
of duties, and the cultivation of talents, peculiar to each, befides thofe
which are incumbent upon all. Reflection upon the fubject will fhew,
that a confiderable degree of intellectual improvement is neceffary,
for females of the fuperior claffes of
fociety, to capacitate them for the
proper application of that influence,
which is conferred on them by their
fitu-

fituation, for the purpofe of promoting the public welfare.

The indifpenfable duties of wives,
mothers, and heads of families, are
incumbent upon all ranks; though it
is not obligatory upon the perfons,
who compofe the clafs under confideration, to execute every office belonging to thefe relations themfelves,
yet it is incumbent on them to in-
fpect the whole; to regulate the plan
of action; and to examine whether
their fubftitutes difcharge their refpective engagements properly. As
wives, the difpofal of that part of
their hufband's revenue, which is
confumed by the family, falls under
their direction, and they are required
to prevent either the profufion of
wafte, or the unbecoming parfimony
of want: As mothers, they are re-

G   fponfible,

fponfible, efpecially, for the religious
and moral education of their children: As miftreffes, the regulation
of the moral conduct of their female
domeftics devolves upon them, and
is a charge which cannot be wholly
tranfmitted to a houfe-keeper. Here
is a wide field for action ; but a much
more extended one lies beyond it.

The female poor in their neighbourhood have undeniable claims
upon them, not only for a liberal diftri-
bution of pecuniary affiftance in cafes
of ficknefs or unavoidable diftrefs, but
alfo for a part of their time, proportioned to their leifure. Without any
impertinent interference with the ex-
clufive departments of men, in the
adminiftration of parochial bufinefs,
there are many important benefits
which might be derived from the

4   co-

co-operation of women of enlarged
underftandings, in the fuperintend-
ence of the poor of their own fex.
Delicacy, tendernefs, practical fkill
in their concerns, and fympathizing
in their fufferings, eminently qualify
women for the tafk. The patronage
and management of ufeful inftitutions for the improvement of their
morals, and the increafe of their happinefs, the infpection of workhoufes,
fchools of induftry, and cottages, not
merely once or twice in a twelve-
month, but fo frequently as to become acquainted with the wants and
condition of the inhabitants, would
enable women of the higher claffes
to do much good, and to correct
many abufes, of which men are feldom competent judges; particularly
with refpect to the rearing of chil-

dren,

dren, and the prefervation of the
morals of female parifh apprentices.
It is a fact too well attefted to need
farther evidence, that the lives of
thoufands of infants have been loft
in poorhoufes, from negleCt, feverity, and mifmanagement. Policy,
as well as humanity, fuggefts the
propriety of adopting fome meafure
likely to check this enormous evil,
and diminifh fuch a dreadful wafte
of human life. An appointment of
female vifitors, empowered to examine, and make report weekly or
monthly, of the ftate of the infants in
the workhoufe, in each parifh through-
out the kingdom, might produce
effeCtual reformation, and contribute
to the general order of the reft of the
inmates of thefe houfes of affliCtion.
The fenfibility of the fex does not
admit

admit a doubt, but that there might
be found a fufficient number to re-
lieve each other, in every parifh, who
would willingly overcome the difficulties of fuch an undertaking, in
the caufe of thefe innocent fufferers.
Workhoufes, in their prefent ftate,
it muft be acknowledged, are but too
generally places of difguft and loath-
fomenefs; but a conftant recurrence
of thefe vifits would moft probably
render them cleaner, and lefs offen-
five to the feelings of humanity.

The apprentices bound out by a
parifh, and girls difcharged from
charity fchools at the very age when
they moft need the protection of a
guardian, are objects of peculiar
commiferation: The former are
frequently configned to the mercy
of a mafter, who is either vicious or

cruel;

cruel; in the one cafe, they fall innocent victims to his irregular paffions; and in the other are fubjected,
with unreafonable feverity, to tafks
too hard to be performed. Was
each girl apprenticed by a parifh, to
be placed under the infpection of one
or two of the moft refpectable female inhabitants, it would not only
reftrain the ill conduct of the mafter
or miftrefs, but likewife ftimulate the
child to behave herfelf fo as to deferve the future patronage of her
fuperiors. The care beftowed upon
girls in charity-fchools of all defcrip-
tions, is of little avail, if they are
difmiffed at a certain age, without
creditable fituations being provided
for them. After feveral years of inftruction, it is a common practice to
abandon them wholly to the management

ment of their parents, who from being unable to maintain them, are glad to let them to the firft place that offers, without the leaft difcrimination into the charaćter of their employers. Would the patroneffes of fuch fchools extend their benevolent care for the fpace of a few more years, in tracing the children from place to place, and rewarding thofe who deferved it, by recommendation and fome fmall teftimony of their approbation, it would complete the plan of bringing up fuch children to be ufeful members of the community; and there is little doubt but the fuccefs would be adequate to their hopes. The life of one infant, or the prefervation of one innocent girl from perdition, would be a recompence worth any trouble the attempt might incur.

The

The reformation of vice, the inftruction of ignorance, and the promotion of virtue, are among the moft
dignified occupations of the human
intellect; but noble and interefting
as they are, they lie within the com-
pafs of female underftanding, and
if affiduoufly purfued, will fill up the
vacancies of a life of leifure, with
honour, profit, and pleafure. The
example of the worthy Hanway in
the difpofal of his time, deferves imitation: He remarks, that he did not
leave works of benevolence to accidental opportunity, but that he was
accuftomed to allot a fpecific part of
his time to the exprefs purpofe. It
is an admirable practice to divide the
day into regular portions, appropri-
ating them to their refpective claims,
in order that duties, ftudies, and
amufe-

amufements may each have their proportionate fhare of attention, and not intrude upon one another.

The duties of an elevated rank are very extenfive, as has been already fhewn, but if hours are properly œconomifed they will not abforb them all, but a fufficient opportunity will be left for the cultivation of the intellectual faculties, and likewife for the enjoyment of temperate pleafure.

After the performance of duties, the improvement of the mind holds the fecond place. The tafte of individuals alone can direct the choice in felect-ing congenial objects from amongft the innumerable fcientific purfuits, which adorn, and add a luftre to the moft diftinguifhed fituations. What-ever has a tendency to ftrengthen the judgment, to enlarge the com-

pafs

pafs of the underftanding, to imprefs
juft principles of action, and raife the
mind to the contemplation of the
wifdom of the Creator, by an acquaintance with his works, deferves
a decided preference. The acquifition of languages, fimple mathematics, aftronomy, natural and ex-
perimental philofophy, with hiftory
and criticifm, may be cultivated by
the fex with propriety and advantage, according to their different
degrees of induftry and perfeverance.

The lighter ftudies, which muft
alfo depend upon tafte, may, not improperly, clafs amongft amufements.
Here a variety of delightful objects
prefent themfelves to the imagination, offered by the fine arts, and
their innumerable elegant productions.

tions. Poetry, mufic, painting, and
ftatuary are fources of the moft refined entertainment; whether our
admiration is excited by thofe choice
works of art, which are preferved as
exifting records of the fuperior pro-
ficiency of Greek and Italian artifts;
or whether we ftudy the theory of
thofe principles by which they were
guided to excellence. Should any
one be deprived, by a natural deficiency of tafte, of enjoying the gratification thefe purfuits afford, there
are others, productive of great variety and amufement, which will
probably be more confonant to their
turn of mind. A knowledge of the
cuftoms and manners of different
nations, geography, chemiftry, elec-
tricity, botany, an inveftigation of
the properties and habits of the feveral

veral orders of animals, gardening, turning, and works of ingenuity, may each in fucceffion fill up a leifure opportunity with innocence and ufefulnefs, and become a pleafing antidote to the indolent habit of loitering away time in an unprofitable manner, or what is worfe in diffipation; and fhould thefe recreations encroach upon the vigils of the card-table, the injury to fociety will not be great.

Without inftituting an inquiry into the propriety of this diverfion, or enumerating the evils which frequently attend its excefs, it may appear only confiftent with a work, written exprefsly upon the importance of ufeful employment, to remark the confumption of time expended in it, which may fairly be calculated at one eighth of the day

of

of the majority of the female fex above thirty, who compofe what is termed the genteel world. But to return from this digreffion, to the fubject of pleafures and amufements; a fubject upon which there is great diverfity of opinions, according to prejudice, habit, and education.

The love of pleafure is a dangerous propenfity, and fhould be reftricted within very moderate limits. Its purfuit may be rendered abfolutely unlawful in two ways, both as it refpects the kind, and the quantity; the criterion of expediency in the firft cafe confifts in its perfect innocency; thofe things which are likely to corrupt the purity of the mind, and the affections, are at leaft dangerous, and cannot be authorized by fafhion or example; for it is more than probable,

bable, that fhe who ventures upon the confines of vice, will not efcape uninjured. An extreme diffipation is one of the characteriftic vices of the prefent times; great vigilance, therefore, is neceffary in high life to reftrain its excefs : whatever injures the health, intrudes upon more important avocations, or incurs an immoderate expence, well deferves the appellation of exceffive and unjuftifiable. Judged by thefe rules, a frequent attendance upon places of public diverfion will ftand condemned ; and in whatever point of view it is examined, it will be found wholly incompatible with that purity of character, which is the effence of female perfection. The incontrovertible oppofition between what is denominated a life of pleafure, and one of religion,

religion, and habits of moral virtue,
has been fo often, and fo ably proved
by the moft refpectable authors,
efpecially by thofe who have written
particularly for the female fex, that
it feems unneceffary to enter into a
difcuffion of it here. But there is
another motive for fubjecting the
inordinate purfuit of pleafure within
the bounds of moderation, which,
though likely to prevail with a mind
truly magnanimous and patriotic,
has not been fo often urged, and is
peculiarly incumbent upon thofe,
whofe elevated fphere of action gives
an impreffive force to their example.
Women are prohibited from the
public fervice of their country by
reafon and decorum, but they are
not excluded from promoting its
welfare by other means, better
adapted

adapted to their powers and attainments. The gradual and almoſt imperceptible, though certain influence of forming the opinions, and improving the manners of their countrywomen, by their converſation and their practice, is the undiſputed prerogative of our female nobility. Should one of that order, inſtead of yielding to the torrent of faſhion, uſe the influence of her rank, to check the increaſing and pernicious ſpirit of diſſipation; ſhould ſhe avail herſelf of the weight of her own example, to promote a ſobriety of conduct, and the general uſefulneſs of her ſex, the good effects it might produce upon ſociety, would extend beyond her warmeſt expectations: The benefit would indeed be incalculable: Many of thoſe who are her

equals

equals by birth, would be induced to imitate fo noble a model of true greatnefs of mind ; and experience proves that their inferiors will follow wherever they lead.—The civic crown was the reward of any Roman who preferved the life of a fellow-citizen; but how much more worthy of the gratitude of the community would fhe be, who unfubdued by the temptations offered by affluence and high birth, fhould reject them with an heroic magnanimity, and devote her time, her talents, and her fortune, to the improvement of public morals, and the increafe of public happinefs.

The employments already fuggefted remove every complaint of a deficiency of materials for the exercife of the faculties or the fancy,

H   and

and leave no room for vapoured idlenefs to lament the tedioufnefs of time.
Whilft to greatnefs is annexed the
privilege of forming and patronizing
inftitutions of utility to reward genius, to raife and to protect modeft
worth, languifhing in obfcurity, to
encourage manufactures, to countenance, in an efpecial manner, the
induftry of their own fex, in every
department in which they can be
employed, and to ufe the moft ftre-
nuous efforts to remove thofe prejudices, which have a tendency to
continue women in a ftate of ignorance, diffipated floth, inactivity, and
helplefs dependance.

CHAPTER V.

On the Duties, Studies, and Amusements of Women of the second class in Society.

THE virtues, purfuits, and amufements of a diftinguifhed condition, partake of the publicity of that ftation; thofe of a contracted fphere, are lefs expofed to obfervation; but as they contribute to increafe or to diminifh the fum of general happinefs, they fhould alfo be regulated upon principles of reafon, inftead of being abandoned to the direction of accidental impreffions.

As it is not to be fuppofed, that many individuals of that order of women, who clafs next in rank and confequence to the one already dif-cuffed, draw their refources from

H 2   here-

hereditary poſſeſſions, the contingency of ſupply is more uncertain, and implicates a greater probability of a change in circumſtances ; on which account, the exerciſing a well-ordered œconomy, and of acquiring the art of managing the expenditure of the income in the moſt advantageous manner is apparent, and generally devolves upon the female partner, whoſe acquirements in youth ſhould therefore be directed to objects of utility, in preference to thoſe which are merely ornamental.

Domeſtic duties ſtand diſtinguiſhed as pre-eminently uſeful ; a moderate ſituation requires that they ſhould be diſcharged in perſon, an avocation which cannot be judiciouſly performed, without conſiderable knowledge and attention. The

art

art of œconomifing and rendering
all kinds of food as palatable and
nourifhing as poffible, by different
modes of cookery, will repay the
miftrefs of a houfhold for the trouble of inveftigation, and fhould in-
difputably form a part of the regular
inftruction of girls of the middle
rank, to which, as they advance towards maturity, may profitably be
added a knowledge of the value of
all neceffary articles confumed in a
family, whether for the table or the
wardrobe, as well as the quantities
of each which are requifite for refpective ufes. As theory is of little
avail, unlefs exemplified by practice,
they fhould be habituated to exercife
the department of houfe-keeper under the infpection of their mother,
not only by purchafing the different

com-

commodities wanted for the ufe of
the family, but likewife by keeping
an exact account of the domeftic
expences, which will afford opportunities of teaching them a judicious
application of money, and giving
them diftinct ideas, where frugality may moft properly be exerted,
and where greater, latitude may be
allowed. Neither will fome information concerning the ufe of domeftic
medicine, or kitchen phyfic, as it is
called, be without its advantage, as
well as fkill in preparing broths and
other things for the fick ; nor fhould
the management of a fick chamber,
to the attendance of which women
are fo often called, be left to the un-
certainty of inexperience; girls fhould
be initiated in the beft methods of
alleviating the fufferings, and contri-

4   buting

buting to the comfort of thofe who are indifpofed.

Where there are younger children in the fame family, the inviting opportunity of inftructing them in the moft rational fyftem of bringing up infants fhould not be neglected; for what can be more ridiculous, and at the fame time more common, than to fee a young woman become a mother, who fcarcely knows how to handle a baby, and who would be alarmed at the thoughts of dreffing one. Inftruction and previous experience, are thought abfolutely neceffary to qualify us for the difcharge of almoft every office, except that of the parental character; but, alas! the duties of this very important relation, the confequences of which extend even to a future generation,

are

are left to be discovered by accident, as the occasions for performing them arise.

The functions of domestic life occupy a considerable portion of time, even under the regulation of the most methodical arrangement, but as they are of indispensable obligation, the hours they consume need not be regretted: Order, precision, and a thorough knowledge of the different family concerns, will however expedite the accomplishment of this essential business, and leave sufficient opportunity for other avocations. The only satisfactory apology which can be made for transferring the management of children, or the cares of the houshold, to others, is a devotion of that time, which would otherwise be their due, to

some

fome means of procuring refources to maintain them. But even when the miftrefs of a family is thus profitably engaged, every domeftic department fhould be regulated by her orders, and be conducted under her infpection: The eye of a judicious manager pervades every object, and at a glance regulates the whole; efpecially if her fervants be upright and well-intentioned, and fhe have learnt the happy art of winning their affections: For a ready obedience is the fruit of attachment, and is the axis upon which the order of a family principally turns.

There are many lines of bufinefs in which a wife is capable of affifting her hufband, and wherever a man follows an occupation that can poffibly be tranfacted by a woman, it is

a pre-

a precaution of prudence, againſt
the accident of his death, to inſtruct
his wife in the ſecrets of his profeſſion; even ſhould the eaſe of his
circumſtances preclude the neceſſity
of her taking an active part in it
during his life Some men may
probably diſpute the propriety of
making their wives too well acquainted with their affairs, they may
ſuppoſe, that it will tend to make
them arrogant and preſuming with
regard to expence; or they may be
unwilling to confide to their prudence, the knowledge of private
concerns unfit for general communication. The plain anſwer to theſe
cavils is, that men ſhould not marry
women who are unworthy of their
confidence; and that in a well-found-
ed marriage, intereſt is indiviſible;

that

that alfo, from the fuperior purity of
the morals of women, and the ex-
quifite tendernefs of mothers for their
offspring, as well as from the timi-
dity of the female character, there·is
great reafon to believe, that many
families might have been refcued
from ruin, had the boldnefs of fpecu-
lation, or the imprudence of adven-
ture in the hufband, been reftrained
by the temperate views of the wife.
But, above all, the improvement
that is daily gaining ground in the
education of women, authorizes a
prefumption that they will gradually
become adapted to ferious occupations, and that as they advance in
ufeful knowledge, and the exercife
of·their reafoning powers, they will
obtain a more implicit confidence
from their hufbands, and will be regarded

garded by them as the friend of their
bosoms, rather than as the mere
companion of their hours of recreation. Another general argument
may still be urged to remove the
jealous apprehension of men, lest,
that by teaching women too much,
and by rendering them too useful,
they should become independent of
them: That as a more rational education prevails, women will be better
acquainted with their relative situation, and as their ideas are more defined, they will perceive, that there
can be but one head or chief in every
family; nature and reason, as well
as custom, have established this power
in the hands of the men; therefore,
so far from puffing them up, and
making them self-willed or presump-
tuous, an increase of real knowledge
will

will conduce to give them a juſt eſti-
mate of what they owe to themſelves,
and what is due to their huſbands;
it will not teach them a ſervile un-
qualified obedience, ſuch as can only
be obſerved by ſlaves, for that is
an abſurdity in a connection which
involves the mutual happineſs of
two perſons, but it will promote a
diffidence of their own judgment in
concerns of moment, and an habitual
reference, on ſuch occaſions, to the
more enlarged experience of mankind in their huſbands. Thus the
effects of an enlightened underſtand-
ing, will be found directly contrary to
thoſe which are ſuppoſed to ariſe
from it by a narrow policy.

There are other employments
which may laudably occupy that
time, which can be ſpared from the
important

important engagements of domeſtic
duties, among which the active offices of benevolence demand a pre-
cedence; for women of the ſecond
claſs are not exonerated from uſing
every means that their ſituation affords, of relieving the miſeries of
thoſe who are placed in a ſtate of
poverty, from the obligation incumbent upon the firſt, of taking the
lead in the promotion and ſuperin-
tendence of charitable inſtitutions.
Neither will mediocrity of circumſtances be an adequate apology for
the neglect of this duty : a little money well applied, goes a great way
in alleviating the diſtreſſes of the
indigent; beſides, pecuniary aid is not
the only aſſiſtance, nor always the
beſt that may be extended to them.
Time and perſonal exertion, are in
many

many cafes more powerful agents
for relieving their fufferings. Numberlefs are the modes by which the
well informed may contribute to
the comfort and affiftance of thofe,
who have no fixed principles of
action. In addition to the religious and moral inftruction of the
poor, advice may be valuable to
them, in teaching them how to cut
out their clothes; to give the beft
relifh to their homely fare; to apply
fimple medicines to the fick; to regulate the difpofal of their fmall pittance to the beft advantage; to procure an increafe of comfort, by a
greater degree of cleanlinefs, order,
and good management. To advice
may be united confolation, and the ex-
preffion of that tender fympathy, which
binds man to man, from a partici-
pation

pation of the fame nature; and would, if the voice of humanity were not ftifled by indolence, avarice, and pride, cement the whole human race into one brotherhood.

But the miftrefs of a family may alfo find many opportunities of exercifing thefe affections, in the inftruction of her fervants and dependants, in all the branches of ufeful knowledge that are adapted to their ftation: the promotion of our own intereft, if duly confidered, as well as a folicitude for their welfare, fhould be an inducement to improve them in whatever will enable them to perform the functions of their fituation with more propriety and effect; ignorance, rather than ill-intention, is the frequent caufe of their faults; they are carelefs, wafteful, irregular, and

and imperfect in almost every thing they do, from want of information, and habits of order in their childhood; upon which account there are few services, that can be rendered to the public, by a private individual of our sex, more beneficial than that of taking a poor child into her family, and forming her into a useful servant, at the age when they are commonly discharged from charity schools, and exposed to all the evils of bad example at home, or the unfavourable impressions of a low place. The persons who are best suited to engage in this benevolent attempt, are those whose unincumbered situation gives them opportunity to devote a considerable portion of leisure to the execution of it: in order to succeed, they should remember,

I

member, that the object of their en-
gaging in it, is not merely their own
accommodation, but also to serve
the child they have patronized, and
to fulfil a part of that obligation to
do good, which is enforced upon all
by the doctrines of christianity.
Founded upon such principles, dif-
cipline will be tempered with patience, and they will not grow weary
of the task before it is completed.
How effectually would such persons
perfect the design of the patrons of
schools of industry, whose work requires to be continued under another
form, till the children they have refcued from ignorance have attained
maturity.

Living examples are not wanting
to encourage activity in the cause of
humanity, for the present age abounds

in

in excellent characters, especially of
the female sex, who have contri-
buted very confiderably to the civilization of the poor. The ufeful
works of Mrs. Trimmer; the inge-
nious defign' of Mifs Hannah More,
in the publication of the cheap repofitory for the diffufion of religious
and civil knowledge; and the repofitory for fine works, contrived by
the delicate fenfibility of the honour-
ble Mrs. Cooper, as a mart for the
fale of the labours of thofe, whom
a fenfe of former profperity, con-
ceals from the eye of obfervation *,

are

* The repofitory for fine works, is an inftitution
for the reception and difpofal of any production,
from a pair of knit garters, to the moft elegant
works of ingenuity. The price of each article,
and a number, are affixed to it, by which the
name of the owner is concealed. This eftablifh-

ment

are teſtimonies of the capacity of women, to convert that leiſure, which is ſo commonly devoted to mere amuſement, to purpoſes of real utility, without derogating from that purity and decorum, which peculiarly characterize the ſex.

The education of the girls belonging to this claſs eſpecially, would anſwer the purpoſes of life more effectually, were their attention confined to a ſmaller compaſs of attainments, which ſhould be taught ſcientifically, and application to them continued, until a perfect knowledge of them is obtained. It is a too general error in female inſtruction, to aim

iment deſerves the patronage of the public, both on account of the utility of its deſign, and the variety and taſte diſplayed in the articles to be ſeen there.—The ſhop is at No. 22, Haymarket.

at

at the acquifition of numerous accomplifhments, without ever becoming an adept in any one ; to which
caufe may partly be attributed the
helplefs and lamentable fituation of
women, when the fmiles of profperity are withdrawn, and they are left
to ftruggle with the diftreffing, and,
as things now ftand, the almoft im-
practicable neceffity of procuring for
themfelves a fubfiftence.

In forming a fyftem of inftruction
for the daughters of perfons in the
middle rank, a felection fhould be
made of thofe ftudies, which require
the fmalleft confumption of time, and
which are likely to contribute to ufefulnefs, tending rather to reprefs, than
to encourage, propenfities towards
diffipation and extravagance, exercifing the rational faculties, and pre-

paring

paring them to be capable of defin-
ing the duties required of them in
the various allotments of their future lives: without prefuming to
enumerate or limit the peculiar arts
and fciences fuitable for them to
learn, there are fome, which from
their eminent utility deferve to
be recommended. A grammatical
knowledge of the Englifh language,
and an intimate acquaintance with
the beft authors, who have excelled
in hiftory, biography, poetry, and
morality, are indifpenfable. Simple
mathematics are fo advantageous, in
accuftoming the mind to method
both in reafoning and practice, that
it is to be greatly defired that they
more generally compofed a part of
female education; arithmetic efpecially, and the knowledge of book-
keeping,

4

keeping, fhould be taught funda-
mentally, as the means of contributing to the fuccefs of any bufinefs,
undertaken in cafe of neceffity.—
Drawing, not merely for the purpofe of making pleafing pictures,
and obtaining applaufe, but for that
capacity it gives to a proficient of
reprefenting any object with eafe and
accuracy, is both an ufeful and amuf-
ing qualification; nor are its good
effects confined to the exercife of the
art alone, it ftrengthens the habit of
obfervation, and facilitates the acquifition of natural hiftory, which
is a ftudy at once delightful and valuable; and it promotes a reverential
admiration of the wifdom and goodnefs of the Great Firft Caufe.

The diverfions of this order fhould
partake of the moderation of their

rank,

rank, and be restrained by a limited
application of time and expence; the
mind certainly requires relaxation,
but judgment should be used in the
choice of such amusements as are
consistent with our situation : the
poignancy of enjoyment, is not mea-
sured by the costliness of the object
which produces it. The pleasures
of select society afford an innocent
and delightful resource from more
serious occupation, and very desir-
ably fill up many of the chasms
which arise, even in a busy life: con-
versation sharpens the understand-
ing, and may be modelled into one
of the most agreeable vehicles of instruction. Books are the best sub-
stitutes for the charms of society;
they amuse the imagination, and enrich the mind with knowledge, when
company

company cannot be collected: to
thofe who love reading, a rational
amufement is never wanting; for;
amidft the diverfified talents of Englifh writers, from Milton to Peter
Pindar, every tafte may find congenial
entertainment. Innumerable are the
purfuits, to which a mind liberally
inftructed, may recur for the indulgence of fancy, or the more ferious employment of the intellectual
powers. Nature prefents a rich har-
veft to thofe, who know how to efti-
mate her pure pleafures: the contemplation of her productions, from
the moft lowly plant to the magni-
ficent luminary that enlightens our
fphere, fupplies a never-failing ftore
of entertainment, unmixed with the
pangs of felf-reproach, or the bitter-
nefs of repentance. Opportunities
will

will occur when the mind may be
fuffered to unbend, and yield to the
invitations of pleafure unmixed with
improvement; but thefe recreations
fhould not return too often, left indulgence fhould create a zeft for
diffipation, not eafily extinguifhed,
and weaken the inclination for thofe
purfuits, which have a fuperior claim
to attention.

The choice of amufements is a teft,
which will always diftinguifh a folid
from a fuperficial underftanding; for
thofe pleafures which have no other
merit, than that of paffing away time
harmlefsly, may pleafe the unreflect-
ing; but will not fatisfy minds of a
higher order, who feek for fomething
more productive, even in thefe hours
devoted to relaxation.

CHAPTER VI.

Lucrative Employments for the first and second classes suggested, recommending as agreeable means of procuring a respectable support,— Literature.—Paintings; Historic, Portrait, and Miniature.— Engraving.— Statuary.— Modelling. — Music. —Landscape. — Garden ing.—With Strictures on a Theatrical Life.

TRANSITIONS in private life from affluence to poverty, like the fable pageantry of death, from their frequency, produce no lasting impreſſions upon the beholders. Unexpected misfortunes befal an acquaintance, who has been careſſed in the days of proſperity; the change is lamented, and ſhe is confoled by the viſits of her friends, in the firſt moments of affliction: ſhe finks gradually into wretchedneſs; ſhe becomes

comes obfcure, and is forgotten. The
cafe would be different, could avocations be fuggefted, which would
enable thefe, who fuffer fuch a re-
verfe of fortune, to maintain a de-
cent appearance, and procure them
a degree of refpect. It is far from
my prefent defign, to point out all
the various purfuits which may confiftently engage the talents, or employ the induftry of women, whofe refinement of manners unfit them for
any occupation of a fordid menial
kind; fuch an undertaking would require an extenfive acquaintance with
the diftinct branches of the fine arts,
which adorn, and of the numerous
manufactures which enrich, this country. But a few remarks upon the
nature of thofe employments, which
are beft adapted to the higher claffes

of

of the fex, when reduced to necef-
fitous circumftances, may, perhaps,
afford ufeful hints to thofe, who are
languifhing under the preffure of
misfortune, and induce abler pens to
treat a fubject hitherto greatly neglected.

Numerous difficulties arife in the
choice of occupations for the purpofe. They muft be fuch as are
neither laborious nor fervile, and
they muft of courfe be productive,
without requiring a capital.

For thefe reafons, purfuits which
require the exercife of intellectual,
rather than bodily powers, are generally the moft eligible.

Literature affords a refpectable
and pleafing employment, for thofe
who poffefs talents, and an adequate
degree of mental cultivation. For
                                although

although the emolument is precarious, and seldom equal to a maintenance, yet if the attempt be tolerably
successful, it may yield a comfortable
assistance in narrow circumstances,
and beguile many hours, which might
otherwise be passed in solitude or
unavailing regret. The fine arts
offer a mode of subsistence, congenial to the delicacy of the most refined
minds, and they are peculiarly adapted
by their elegance, to the gratification
of taste. The perfection of every
species of painting is attainable by
women, from the representation of
historic facts, to the minute execution
of the miniature portrait, if they will
bestow sufficient time and application for the acquisition of the principles of the art, in the study of those
models, which have been the means
of transmitting the names and character

racter of fo many men, to the admiration of pofterity. The fuccefs-
ful exercife of this imitative art requires invention, tafte and judgment:
in the two firft, the fex are allowed
to excel, and the laft may be obtained by a perfeverance in examin-
ing, comparing, and reflecting upon
the works of thofe mafters, who have
copied nature in her moft graceful
forms.

Compared with the numbers of
the other fex, it does not appear that
many females, either in ancient or
modern times, have rendered themfelves celebrated in this line of excellence; but the caufe of this difproportion may furely, with greater
probability, be attributed to its having been attempted by fo few women, than to incapacity; among the
very

very fmall number of female artifts,
who have practifed painting as a
profeffion, there have not been wanting fome inftances of rare merit.
But it is to the genial influence of
education only, that fociety muft
ftand indebted for the frequent recurrence of fuch examples: rare,
indeed, is that genius which over-
comes all obftacles; too often do the
powers of the mind, like the undif-
covered diamond in the mine, lie
dormant, if they be not called forth
by a propitious combination of circumftances. As it is not cuftomary
for girls to ftudy the art of painting,
with a view to adopt it as a profeffion, it is impoffible to afcrrtain the
extent of their capacity for the pencil; but certainly there appears no
natural deficiency, either mental or
corporeal,

corporeal, to prevent them from becoming proficients in that art, were
the bent of their education favourable to the attempt. It muſt be allowed, that within the laſt twenty
years, it has been a general faſhion
for young ladies to learn to draw,
and that it is not unuſual to ſee per-
formances executed in ſuch a manner
as to excite a reaſonable expectation
that their powers, if properly cultivated, would produce teſtimonials of
no inferior ability. But as the view
of the generality is only elegant
amuſement, they do not endeavour
to attain any degree of excellence,
beyond that of copying prints or
drawings ; original deſign is too ar-
duous, and it is conceived that the
qualifications it requires, would en-
groſs too large a portion of time.

K   They

They neither read thofe books which
treat of the fubject in a fcientifie
manner ; they do not affociate with
thofe perfons, whofe converfation is
adapted to form their tafte, nor have
they an opportunity of imbibing the
enthufiafm, which is produced by the
contemplation of the precious models
of antiquity. No furprife can therefore be excited, that thofe fruits are
not vifible, which are the effects of
fuch neceffary preparation.

But as neither exalted genius, nor
the means of cultivating that portion
of it which nature has beftowed, to
the utmoft extent, are likely to be
very generally poffeffed ; it is fortu-
nate for thofe who are lefs liberally
endowed, that there are many profitable, though inferior branches of defign,

fign, or of arts connected with it. The drapery and landfcape both of portraits and hiftorical pieces, are often entrufted to the pupils of the mafter, and conftitute a branch of the art, for which women might be allowed to be candidates. The elegant as well as the humorous defigns which embellifh the windows of print-fellers, &c. alfo fketches for the frontifpieces of books, and other ornaments of the fame kind, muft employ many artifts, nor does it appear that any good reafon for confining them to one fex has been affigned.

Colouring of prints is a lucrative employment; there was a few years ago in London, a French woman, who had a peculiar method of applying water colours to prints, by which fhe might have gained a very

liberal

liberal income, had her industry and
morals been equal to her ingenuity.
Designs for needle-work, and ornamental works of all kinds, are now
mostly performed by men, and those
who have a good taste, obtain a great
deal of money by them; but surely
this employment is one, among many,
which has been improperly assumed
by the other sex, and should be appropriated to women. The delicate
touches of miniature painting, and
painting in enamel, with devices for
rings and lockets in hair-work, are
more characteristic of female talents
than of masculine powers. The de-
lineation of animals or plants for
books of natural history, and colouring of maps or globes may be fol-
lowed with some advantage. Pat-
terns for calico-printers and paper-

I   stainers

ftainers are lower departments of the
fame art, which might furely be allowed as fources of fubfiftence to
one fex with equal propriety as to
the other.

Engraving, though it differ from
painting in the execution, may be
faid to have the fame origin, both
being regulated by fimilar principles,
as far as relates to defign and fhadow ;
therefore, if the faculties of women
are capable of directing the pencil,
there can be no apprehenfion that
they are not alfo equal to guide the
graver with the fame fuccefs.

Statuary and modelling are arts
with which I am too little acquainted
to hazard any opinion concerning,
but the productions of the honourable Mrs. Damer, and a few
others, authorize an affurance, that

K 3   women

women have only to apply their
talents to them in order to excel. If
the refiftance of marble and hard
fubftances be too powerful for them
to fubdue, wax and other materials
of a fofter nature, will eafily yield to
their impreffions. The neceffity of
vigour and perfeverance in cultivating natural talents, is equally great
in attaining perfection of any kind.
The fame remarks which have been
made upon that fubject, with refpect
to painting, are equally applicable to
mufic. Compofition affords an ample fupport to many profeffors, and
depends rather upon a fine tafte, and
a theoretic knowledge of the powers
of harmony, more than upon a deep
underftanding or philofophical re-
fearch. The names of celebrated
female compofers are probably ftill
more

more rare than thofe of female paint-
ers; for the fcarcity of the latter we
have already endeavoured to account,
and fimilar reafons may be affigned
for the former.

The ftage is a profeffion, to which
many women of refined manners,
and a literary turn of mind have had
recourfe. Since it has been cuftomary for females to affume dramatic
characters, there appears to have
been full as great a proportion of
women, who have attained celebrity,
among thofe who have devoted
themfelves to a theatrical life, as of
the other fex; a fact which argues
that there is no inequality of genius,
in the fexes, for the imitative arts;
the obfervation may operate as a
ftimulant to women to thofe purfuits
which are lefs objectionable than the

ftage;

ftage; which is not mentioned for the
purpofe of recommending it, but of
proving that the abilities of the female fex are equal to nobler labours
than are ufually undertaken by women. The profeffion of an actrefs is
indeed moft unfuitable to the fex in
every point of view, whether it be
confidered with refpect to the courage
requifite to face an audience, or the
variety of fituations incident to it,
which expofe moral virtue to the
moft fevere trials. Let the daughters of a happier deftiny, whilft they
lament the evils to which fome of
their fex are expofed, remember
thofe unpropitious circumftances,
that have caft them into a line of life,
in which it is fcarcely poffible to
preferve that purity of fentiment and
conduct, which characterizes female
excel-

excellence. When their errors are difcuffed, let the harfh voice of cen-fure be reftrained, by the reflection, that fhe who has made the greateft advances towards perfection, might have fallen, had fhe been furrounded by the fame influences.

That fpecies of agriculture which depends upon fkill in the manage-ment of the nurfery-ground, in rear-ing the various kinds of fhrubs and flowers, for the fupply of gentle-men's gardens and pleafure grounds, would fupply an elegant means of fupport to thofe women who are able to raife a capital for carrying on a work of that magnitude. Ornamen-tal gardening, and the laying out of pleafure grounds and parks, with the improvement of natural landfcape, one of the refinements of modern times,

times, may likewife afford an eligible maintenance to fome of thofe females, who in the days of their profperity, difplayed their tafte in the embellifhment of their own domains.

The prefiding over feminaries for female education, is likewife a fuitable employment for thofe, whofe minds have been enlarged by liberal cultivation, whilft the under parts of that profeffion may be more fuitably filled by perfons whofe early views have been contracted within narrower limits. After all that can be fuggefted by general remarks, the different circumftances of individuals muft decide the profeffion moft convenient to them. But it is a confolatory reflection, that amidft the daily viciffitudes of human life, from which no rank is exempt, there are refources, from which aid may be drawn, without derogating from the true dignity of a rational being.

CHAPTER VII.

On the duties, attainments, and employments of Women of the third Class.—Censuring the giving of greater rewards to Men than Women, for similar exertions of time, labour, and ingenuity; and the necessity there is for ladies of rank encouraging their own sex.—Recommending the teaching girls, the serving of retail shops; the undertaking for the female sex; turnery, and farming, as eligible means of support; with an extract from Sir F. M. Eden, of an account of a Female Farmer.

THE next class of women which comes under animadversion, includes several gradations, involving the daughters of every species of tradesmen below the merchant, and above the meaner mechanic: consequently, very different degrees of refinement befit

befit the individuals who form the
extreme links, which are feparated,
infenfibly as it were, from the other
divifions towards which they ap-
proximate. The peculiar duties of
each, will vary according to their
refpective fituations ; but humility,
fobriety, modefty of deportment, an
induftrious difpofition, and an ad-
juftment of their manners to their
circumftances, are the characteriftic
ornaments of their general condition.

The fame caufe, whence originates
a variation in the functions which
they are called to fulfil, will alfo
require different modifications in
their inftruction ; but in a fketch upon
fuch a fubject, as a mere outline only
can be drawn, which may be adapted
to the majority of the perfons for
whom it is defigned, particular diftinctions

tinctions muft be left to the judgment of parents, who fhould be
guided by the profpect of the probable future deftination of their off-
fpring.

Reading fluently, and fpelling cor-
rectly will form a fufficient knowledge
of the Englifh language; and as their
avocations will not admit of an extenfive courfe of reading, the books
felected for them fhould be fuch as
are addreffed to the underftanding,
rather than to the imagination. A
complete acquaintance with the
practical parts of fcripture is effentially
neceffary, and fhould be taught them
daily, as leffons for the conduct of
life*. Plays and novels, with every
work

* The following books are fuitable to form a
part of the library of young women, who have
but little leifure to devote to reading :

Trimmer's

work tending to inflame the paſſions, and implant ſentiments of the omni-potence of love and beauty, ſhould be moſt carefully excluded from their ſight, AS CONTAINING A BANEFUL POISON, DESTRUCTIVE OF EVERY PRINCIPLE THAT IS ADAPTED TO DEFEND THEM FROM THE ALLURE-MENTS OF VICE. The relative ſi-

Trimmer's Bible, with Annotations and Reflec-tions.

Œconomy of Human Life.

Penn's Reflections and Maxims.

Hanway's Virtue in Humble Life.

Sturm's Reflections for every Day in the Year.

Barbauld's Hymns.

Watts's Poems.

A Collection of Poems for young Perſons, by Rachel Barclay.

Aikin's England delineated.

Robinſon Cruſoe.

Trimmer's Family Magazine.

Trimmer's Servant's Friend, and two Farmers.

Hannah More's Repoſitory.

tuation

tuation of the four continents, and
the kingdoms which they contain;
the principal cities, rivers, and moun-
tains of Europe, with the manners
of the different nations, and the produce of each, both natural and artificial, and a more accurate knowledge of the divifions and chief
towns of our own ifland, would form
a ftudy, at once ufeful, entertaining,
and unobjectionable. A general acquaintance with the leading events
of Englifh hiftory, collected from
fome well-written compendium,
might alfo be admitted as an occa-
fional recreation from bufinefs.

Ufeful needlework in every branch,
with complete fkill in cutting out
and making every article of female
drefs, fhould be a principal object in
their inftruction, and ought to employ

ploy a confiderable part of the day in childhood. Arithmetic is a fcience of fuch general application in the concerns of every rank, that it fhould be learnt by all univerfally, who are above the clafs of labourers ; the want of a thorough acquaintance with figures, and a methodical fyftem of book-keeping, have conduced to the ruin of many fmall tradefmen , and as fuch knowledge is more likely to give exact than refined ideas, no dangerous confequences need be apprehended from it; nor would there be ground for alarm to thofe who are apprehenfive of beftowing too much learning upon the inferior ranks, if the inftruction of thofe above penury was extended to the fimpleft elements of geometry, for it is to be prefumed, that the effect of this ac-

L   quifition

quifition would rather qualify than
unfit them for the duties of their ftation. The objects concerning which
thefe fifter fciences treat, being confined to the underftanding, they poffefs nothing in their nature encouraging to perfonal vanity, or to that falfe
pride, which often excites one order
of men to tread too clofely upon the
footfteps of that above them : the
knowledge of things that are in themfelves ufeful, can only be injurious
when it has a tendency to break down
the diftinctions of fociety, by aroufing
a paffion for fcience in the bofoms
of individuals of a certain condition,
which can feldom be gratified but
at the expence of their welfare in
life.

A comparifon of this fyftem of
education with that in frequent ufe
among

among perfons of this defcription,
may effectually remove the prejudices of thofe, who confider the one
propofed as too liberal for the women for whom it is defigned. On
the one hand appears plain inftruction in a plain garb, reading, fpelling,
writing, arithmetic, geometry, ufeful
books, and family needle-work; on
the other appear polite manners, a
fmattering of French and dancing, to
which is fometimes added mufic, em-
broidery, and fine works. From
this picture let the moft adverfe to
their improvement decide, which is
beft calculated to enable them to
difcharge the duties of their ftation.

Civilization would be advanced,
by beftowing fuch a rational mode of
education upon this order of the fex, as
fhall teach them juft notions of their

duties

duties and offices, and of the proper
place they hold in fociety. Ignorance,
and a vague manner of thinking, are
the fprings of many errors in conduct
among them, which are increafed by
pernicious publications, containing
improbable fictions, dreffed up in.
the imagery of glowing language,
filled with falfe fentiments of delicacy
and fenfibility, and prefenting models
of female perfection unfit for their
imitation ; for nothing can be more
diftant from the plain, fober, ufeful
qualities of a houfewife, than the ex-
cellencies of the heroine of a novel.
Errors of opinion are of all kinds the
moft dangerous, as they lead to improper conduct, even when the in-
tentions are upright ; whilft the modeft virtues of induftry, frugality, and
fimplicity of behaviour, are regarded
with

with contempt, in vain will the practice of them be enforced. The refinement of manners and extravagant
appearance of young women of small
expectations is a discouragement to
marriage; for what prudent tradef-
man would venture to burthen him-
felf with a wife, who, by her miftaken
ambition of gentility, would confume
all the produce of his induftry, without contributing her endeavours to
increafe the common ftock. Celibacy, among the inferior ranks efpecially, is a political evil of fuch
magnitude, as to require every check
that wifdom can fuggeft; for whether confidered with reference to individual happinefs and virtue, or the
general good, its confequences are
fatal. The frequency of marriage is
beft promoted by rendering it defir-

able:

able : what can be fo likely to effeＣt
that purpofe, as the bringing up girls
with fuch habits as will fit them
for helpmates.

The knowledge of a trade is a probable means, which ought not to
be negleＣted, of enabling them to
give their affiftance towards the fupport of their family ; but fhould it
be more eligible for the hufband and
the wife to unite in the profecution
of the fame defign, her former fub-
jeＣtion to regular application will render her more apt in accommodating
herfelf to her hufband's bufinefs. Thus
the benefit of apprenticing girls of
this rank to fome trade is equally
apparent, whether they marry or
live fingle.

Men monopolize not only the moft
advantageous employments, and fuch
as

as exclude women from the exercife
of them, by the publicity of their nature, or the extenfive knowledge
they require, but even many of
thofe, which are confiftent with the
female chara&ter. Another heavy
difcouragement to the induftry ot
women, is the inequality of the reward of their labour, compared with
that of men, an injuftice which pervades every fpecies of employment
performed by both fexes *.

* This abufe is in no inftance more confpicu-
ous, than in the wages of domeftic fervants. A
footman, efpecially of the higher kind, whofe moft
laborious talk is to wait at table, gains, including
clothes, vails, and other perquifites, at leaft £. 50
per annum, whilft a cook-maid, who is miftrefs
of her profeffion, does not obtain £. 20, though
her office is laborious, unwhoiefome, and requires
a much greater degree of fkill than that of a va-
let. A fimilar difproportion is obfervable among
the inferior fervants of the eftablifhment.

In

In employments which depend upon bodily ftrength the diftinction is juft; for it cannot be pretended that the generality of women can earn as much as men, where the produce of their labour is the refult of corporeal exertion ; but it is a fubject of great regret, that this inequality fhould prevail, even where an equal fhare of fkill and application are exerted. Male-ftay-makers, mantua-makers, and hair-dreffers are better paid than female artifts of the fame profeffions ; but furely it will never be urged as an apology for this difproportion, that women are not as capable of making ftays, gowns, dreffing hair, and fimilar arts, as men ; if they are not fuperior to them, it can only be accounted for upon this principle, that the prices they

they receive for their labour are not
fufficient to repay them for the expence of qualifying themfelves for
their bufinefs, and that they fink
under the mortification of being regarded as artizans of inferior eftimation, whilft the men, who fupplant
them, receive all the encouragement
of large profits and full employment, which is enfured to them by
the folly of fafhion. The occafion
for this remark is a difgrace upon
thofe who patronize fuch a brood of
effeminate beings in the garb of men,
when fympathy with their humbler
fifters fhould direct them to act in a
manner exactly oppofite, by holding
out every incitement to the induftry
of their own fex. This evil indeed
calls loudly upon women of rank and
fortune for redrefs: they fhould
deter-

determine to employ women only, wherever they can be employed; they should procure female instructors for their children; they should frequent no shops that are not served by women; they should wear no clothes that are not made by them; they should reward them as liberally as they do the men who have hitherto supplanted them. Let it be considered a common cause to give them every possible advantage. For once let fashion be guided by reason, and let the mode sanction a preference to women in every profession, to which their pretensions are equal with those of the other sex. This is a patronage which the necessitous have a right to expect from the rich and powerful, whether they are poor by birth, or are unfortunately become

so

fo by that mutability of fortune to which every rank is liable.

The inftruction of youth in all its various departments offers an eligible means of fupport for thofe women, who have been qualified for the office by fuitable acquirements. A perfon who undertakes to fuperintend the whole of a child or children's education, whether in a private family as governefs, or as the manager of a public feminary, ought to poffefs many rare endowments, and fuch a turn of thinking, and ftyle of behaviour, as are to be gained only by affociation with the beft company. Thofe, therefore, who have been placed in the midft of fuch fociety, by their early profpects, are the only proper candidates for thefe offices. The entire exclufion of men from the teaching

teaching of girls would provide a new species of employment for the daughters of tradesmen, were they to have them completely instructed in any one distinct branch of knowledge which masters teach, with a view of supplying their places. This would ensure them a respectable opportunity of maintaining themselves, should occasion require it, at any period of life, and would be a far more valuable gift than a moderate dowry, which, when once consumed, is irrecoverable, whilst a talent, that can be resumed at discretion, is like a bank, to which application may always be made.

The acquisition of polite accomplishments, unless designed for a profession, should be confined to persons of leisure and superior rank, for they
unfit

unfit others for the duties of their
ftation, by refining their ideas too
much for the fphere in which they
are to act, and giving them a tafte for
a luxurious life and diffipated pleafures, inconfiftent with the happinefs
of themfelves or their connexions. Extenfive knowledge in a particular fcience, or great practical excellence in
one of the fine arts cannot be attained
in the ufual courfe of inftruction at
fchool, therefore fomething like an
apprenticefhip muft be undergone:
a few years, at leaft, after fchool is
left, fhould be devoted to the ftudy
of that art or fcience, which is chofen
for the purpofe, under the direction
of a fkilful profeffor:—For example,
the art of writing, fimple as it is, is
almoft wholly taught by men, becaufe women are incapable of teaching

ing it; but no arguments can be convincing, that they do not poſſeſs a capacity of excelling in penmanſhip, if they beſtowed the ſame application upon it, as thoſe men do, who exerciſe the profeſſion of writing-maſters. The ſame obſervations apply with equal force to the other branches of inſtruction, which are at preſent monopolized by maſters; but if women will have a proper ſpirit to aſſume their rights, and induſtry to qualify themſelves for the exerciſe of them, theſe male intruders will be baniſhed from boarding-ſchools and private families, where the pupils are of the female ſex.

Some remarks are neceſſary upon the ſituation of thoſe, who are precluded by the narrow circumſtances of their parents from being apprenticed.

4

ticed to a trade, or qualified for any
other profeſſion than of upper ſervants in genteel families. Temptations on all ſides frequently beſet
young women thus circumſtanced.
The profligacy of their maſter, or that
of his ſons, is ſometimes their ruin;
but if they eſcape from the attempts
of their ſuperiors, they are expoſed
to the ſociety of a number of idle
lacqueys, whoſe principles are too
commonly vitiated, and their manners corrupted. The neglect of the
miſtreſs, in the moral regulations of
her houſhold, and the influence of
her diſſipated example, frequently in-
creaſe their difficulties in the preſervation of virtuous inclinations and
conduct. The indulgence of their
manner of living diſqualifies them
from becoming uſeful wives to
tradeſ-

tradefmen or artificers, and they have often no other alternative but to remain fingle, or to fubmit to marry a footman and keep a public houfe. This is a melancholy view of their condition; but it might doubtlefs be rendered more comfortable by the confideration of thofe whom they ferve, and upon whom it is incumbent to watch with parental folicitude over the morals of their fervants. The tafk is not eafy, becaufe reformation muft commence with themfelves: a diminution in the number of ufelefs men fervants, who are kept merely for parade, and a determination to retain none, whofe conduct is diforderly, or contrary to the precepts of morality, are fteps neceffary to the advancement of good order in great families.

A fet-

A fettlement in a married ftate, is an enjoyment to which fervants can feldom look forward with any profpect of comfort; and the defpair of attaining it, is doubtlefs a frequent caufe of their libertinifm. A gift or a loan, as the reward of faithful fervices for a certain number of years, to be employed as a capital in fome fmall trade, would be an inducement to fervants to lay up a little ftore as a provifion to enable them to marry. No temporal motive can influence them more powerfully to be moral, fober, frugal, and attached to one mafter, than the hope of exchanging fervitude, though at a diftant day, for an independance, however limited. Though the pleafure of recompenfing a faithful fervant, by an eftablifhment in bufinefs, can

be

be enjoyed only by the opulent, yet
it is poffible for thofe of more contracted poffeffions to contribute to
this defign at a fmaller expence, than
that of advancing a capital. There
may be feveral ways contrived to
encourage them to lay by a part of
their wages, which is one means of
promoting this defign ; many female
fervants, particularly, fquander all
they gain, becaufe they know not
what to do with the fmall fum they
are able to lay by; but if miftreffes
would condefcend to take it into their
hands, and give them intereft for it,
they would be eafily perfuaded to put
by a fmall part of their earnings an-
nually. A part of that fund, which
charity teaches us to believe is
fpared by all for benevolent purpofes, may properly be applied in
rewarding the fidelity of thofe fervants,

vants, who have conducted themfelves well during a feries of years.
Such an attention to promote their
happinefs, would reform that love of
change, and want of attachment, of
which they are fo generally accufed.
The moft effectual precautions,
which a young woman can take,
whofe allotment is fervitude, either
to avoid the evils of a bad place, or
to fecure the advantages of a good
one, are to make a careful enquiry
concerning the moral character of
thofe whofe fervice fhe folicits, before fhe enters into their family; and
to arm herfelf againft the temptation
of high wages, and the appearance
of a genteel fituation, by a refolution
to engage with no perfon, upon any
terms, unlefs they have an eftablifhed reputation for regularity and
decorum.

The

The ſerving of retail ſhops, which
deal in articles of female conſump-
tion, ſhould be excluſively appropriated to women.   For were the multitudes of men, who are conſtantly
employed in meaſuring linen, gauze,
ribbons, and lace ; ſelling perfumes
and coſmetics ; ſetting a value on
feathers and trinkets ; and diſplaying
their talents in praiſing the elegance
of bonnets and caps, to withdraw,
they might benefit the community,
by exchanging ſuch frivolous avocations for ſomething more worthy of
the maſculine character, and by this
meaſure afford an opportunity of
gaining a creditable livelihood to
many deſtitute women, whom a
dreadful neceſſity drives to the buſineſs of proſtitution.—The attendance of women in ſhops, need not be

I   entirely

entirely confined to haberdafhers, perfumers, and milliners; there are other trades in which they may be employed behind the counter: the familiar offices of trying on gloves and fhoes, are more fuitably performed by perfons of the fame fex.

It is wonderful, that amongft the number of modern refinements, an alteration has not been adopted likewife, with refpect to an article of clothing, which cuftom has long placed in the hands of men, at leaft in the vicinity of London, the meafuring and making of which, decency would affign to women. The covering alluded to, by this remark, is the laft which is required. Every undertaker fhould employ women, for the exprefs purpofe of fupplying the female dead, with thofe things

M 3   which

which are requifite. How fhocking
is the idea of our perfons being expofed, even after death, to the obfervation of a parcel of undertaker's
men.

Were it eafier for women to find
employment, or were they brought
up more capable of earning a maintenance, the good effects of fuch a
practice would not be confined to
themfelves alone, but would extend
to the whole community, as it would
be a powerful means of reducing the
number of thofe miferable women,
who fupport a precarious exiftence
by the wages of proftitution, and
who, in their turn, become the fe-
ducers of the inexperienced youth of
the other fex. It would not only
operate as a preventative from devi-
ating into the paths of vice, but
                                    might

might tend to recover fome of thofe who have unfortunately ftrayed. In the prefent ftate of things, if a poor frail unthinking girl yields to the ardent folicitations of the man who has won her affections, and he be fo villainous as to abandon her, fhe is loft without refource, efpecially if fhe be qualified for no occupation but fervice; deprived of character, no perfon will take her into their family; the wants of nature muft be fatisfied, even at the price which produces utter deftruction; and the forlorn deferted one is compelled to betake herfelf to that courfe, which prefently terminates all hope of reftoration to the efteem of others, or to her own approbation.

It is furely unneceffary to infift further upon the benefits of encou-

raging

raging the ufeful induftry of women,
they are too obvious to need a repetition.—Befide thofe employments
which are commonly performed by
women, and thofe already fhewn to
be fuitable for fuch perfons as are
above the condition of hard labour,
there are fome profeffions and trades
cuftomarily in the hands of men,
which might be conveniently exercifed by either fex.—Many parts of
the bufinefs of a ftationer, particularly ruling account books or making
pens. The compounding of medicines in an apothecary's fhop, requires no other talents than care and
exactnefs; and if opening a vein oc-
cafionally be an indifpenfible requifite, a woman may acquire the capacity of doing it for thofe of her
own fex at leaft, without any reafonable

able objection.—Cupping is an art,
which wants neither ftrength in the
performance, nor medical judgment
in the application, as that depends
upon the direction of the phyfician,
and might, under the reftriction juft
mentioned with regard to bleeding,
be exercifed by women.—Paftry and
confectionary appear particularly
confonant to the habits of women,
though generally performed by men:
perhaps the heat of the ovens, and
the ftrength requifite to fill and
empty them, may render male affiftants neceffary ; but certainly women
are moft eligible to mix up the in-
gredients, and prepare the various
kinds of cakes for baking.—Light
turnery and toy-making, depend
more upon dexterity and invention
than

than force, and are therefore fuitable
work for women and children.

There muft be public houfes for
the reception of travellers, and labourers who are fingle, and have no
homes : it were happy indeed for
the community, that they were confined to fuch purpofes, inftead of
being converted into receptacles for
intemperance ; but fince they are neceffary, even in their prefent corrupt
ftate, fome perfons muft fubmit to
the inconveniences of this difagree-
able profeffion. Without recommending it as an eligible employment
for women, reafons may be urged for
the widows of publicans, or even
other women of a certain age, en-
gaging in it ; as houfes of this defcription, which are under female
manage-

management, are generally the moſt orderly, and the moſt ſuccefsful.

Farming, as far as reſpects the theory, is commenſurate with the powers of the female mind ; nor is the practice of inſpecting agricultural proceſſes, incompatible with the delicacy of their frames, if their conſtitution be good. Several inſtances of ſuccefsful female farmers have occurred, and Sir Frederic Morton Eden's opinion confirms the propriety of the practice *. The multiplied

* The following anecdote related in Sir F. M. Eden's ſtate of the poor, exemplifies the idea of it's practicability : ——

" That females are not diſqualified from ſtirring in the moſt active and laborious ſpheres of life, the following intereſting ſketch, which was obligingly communicated to me by a friend, ſeems to afford very ſatisfactory evidence.

" Mrs.

tiplied fources of induftry in a commercial and manufacturing country, rifen to an extraordinary pitch
of

" Mrs. Sarah Spencer was the daughter of
a gentleman in Suffex, her brother having.
once been high fheriff of the county. But her
family, poffeffing only a competent landed eftate,
and being neither engaged, nor in circumftances
to engage, in any lucrative profeffion, like too
many others in this age of univerfal commerce,
infenfibly dwindled to nothing; and though fhe
had been well and genteely educated, and with
fuch views as are common to people in her fphere
of life, yet, on the demife of her father, fhe found
her whole fortune did not amount to quite 300*l.*
Her fifter Mary, a woman of perhaps not inferior
goodnefs of heart, though certainly of very
inferior abilities, was left in a fimilar predicament.
Their perfons, though not uncomely, were not fo
attractive as to flatter them that, without fortune,
they could marry advantageoufly, and a mere
clown was not much more likely to be happy
with them, than they could have been with him.
They either had no relations, on whom they
would have been permitted to quarter themfelves,
or

of refinement, like Britain in the
prefent day, will doubtlefs afford
many other occupations, equally
con-

or they thought fuch a ftate of dependance but a
more fpecious kind of beggary. *Yet, living in
an age and country, in which well educated
women, not born to fortunes, are peculiarly forlorn; with no habits of exertion, nor even of
a rigid frugality, they foon found, that, being thus
unable to work, and afhamed to beg, they had
no profpect but that of pining to death in helplefs and hopelefs penury.* It may he queftioned,
perhaps, whether even the moft refolute fpirits
have virtue enough to embrace a life of labour,
till driven to it by neceffity; but it is no ordinary
effort of virtue, to fubmit to fuch a neceffity with
a becoming dignity. This virtue thefe fifters
poffeffed. At a lofs what elfe to do, they took a
farm, and, without ceafing to be gentlewomen,
commenced farmers. This farm they carried
on for many years, much to their credit and advantage; and, as far as example goes, in an
inftance where example is certainly of moft effect,
not lefs to the advantage of their neighbourhood.
To this day the marks of their good hufbandry
are

confiftent with the female character, as
thofe which have been fuggefted, and
which will occur to perfons of obfervation, who fix their attention upon
the

are to be feen in the village of Rottington. How
is it to be accounted for, without reflecting upon
both the good fenfe and the virtue of thofe perfons in the community, whom a real patriot is
moft difpofed to refpect, I mean the yeomanry
and the peafantry of our villages, it might not be
eafy to fay; but the fact is indifputable, that
thofe who have been moft diftinguifhed for their
endeavours to promote improvements in agriculture, have but rarely been popular characters.
This was the hard fate of the Spencers, who,
inftead of gratitude, long experienced little elfe
than difcourtefies and oppofition in their neighbourhood. The more active of them was called
captain Sally, and her fifter her man Mary.
With the gentry around them, this was not the
cafe; by thefe they were vifited and refpected, as
they deferved to be; and, not feldom, in one and
the fame day, have they divided their hours in
helping to fill the dung-cart, and receiving company of the higheft rank and diftinction. And,
it

the fubject. May a confideration
of finding redrefs for the helpleffnefs
of female indigence, excite a further
enquiry into the moft attainable
means of effecting it.

it was hard to fay, which of thefe offices they
performed with moft intelligence and grace; for,
as has been obferved of Virgil, they even handled
the dung-fork with an air of elegance. To many
of their poorer relations, they were not only
kind, but ufeful. Towards the clofe of their lives,
which happened 14 or 15 years ago, even the
moft perverfe of their neighbours faw their error;
and though they continued not to court popula-
larity, they at length became popular; and
when they died, they were very fincerely regretted."

CHAPTER VIII.

Observations on the condition of the fourth class of Women, suggesting a discrimination in distributing Charity, and an encouragement of Marriage, as a means for its improvement: With remarks on Schools of Industry, and the Houses of the Poor.

T H E manner in which the labouring poor should pass their time, requires but few observations; for their lot dooms them, even in those countries where their situation is most favourable, to incessant toil, as a necessary means of subsistence ; but the rigour of the labour of the female poor should be moderated, by the consideration of their inferiority of strength; and if their condition will admit of improvement, an enquiry into the means most likely to effect it properly, belongs to the subject of these reflections.

The

The internal comfort of a cottage, and the virtues of its inhabitants, depend greatly, if not principally, upon the mother of the family. Œconomy, cleanlinefs, induftry, and, above all thefe, good temper, are the attractions which draw the hufband to his own fire-fide, after the labour of the day is over; but when the wife is flatternly, idle, negligent in providing thofe fmall accommodations, that are the effects of good management, it difcourages him from entrufting her with the difpofal of the wages which he has laborioufly earned, efpecially if to thefe defects be added the intolerable evil of a fcolding tongue, he is driven from home to feek recreation in company, and is too frequently tempted to expend that pittance in excefs, which

N   fhould

ſhould be appropriated to the ſupport of the family.

Very different are the appearances of comfort in the houſes of the poor, according to the management of the wife, even where the earnings are equal: in ſome the children are co-vered with rags, and brought up in the ſtreets to profligacy and ruin; in others, all who are capable of being employed, are buſied in ſome-thing uſeful, proportioned to their age, and their clothes creditably mended to the utmoſt. There is a pretty great certainty, that in thoſe families where neatneſs and induſtry reign, there is no dram drinking, nor any ſcore run up at the chandler's ſhop; for the true œconomiſt will always be in the habit of paying as ſhe goes, well knowing, that if ſhe

4   be

be incapable of difcharging her debts
every week at moft, it will be impoffible to releafe herfelf from the
accumulation of months. If her
hufband brings home his money regularly, fhe contrives to amafs fuch
fums as fhall enable her to buy the
articles of confumption in tolerable
quantities, not by ounces and penny-
worths : a fyftem to which the wafteful prodigal is reduced, by fquan-
dering that fubftance in excefs, or
fuperfluity, which fhould be referved
for the neceffities of the houfhold.

A difcrimination in charitable do-
nations, according to the vifible
effects of good conduct, if generally
adopted by the wealthy, would operate as a ftimulus upon the negligent
to amend, and be a means of aug-
menting the number of comfortable

cot-

cottages: but whilft the bounty of
the rich continues to be beftowed
upon thofe, whofe appearance is the
moft wretched, without allowing
time to enquire whether the caufe of
that exceffive mifery confifts in mifconduct, or unavoidable misfortune;
the importunate, the diffolute, the
idle, and the improvident, will gain
an advantage over the modeft, induftrious, frugal fufferer, who difdains
to folicit compaffion by the artificial
diftrefs of dirt and rags. The mifery
of the poor, like that of other ranks,
chiefly originates in their vices; whatever, therefore, conduces to reform
their morals, will increafe their com-
forts, and improve their condition.
Grofs ignorance, and an infenfibility
to the dignity of their nature, induce
a mean opinion of themfelves, and
stifle

ftifle that worthy confcioufnefs, which
animates the virtuous in the practice
of duty. A juft fenfe of religion is
the only pure foundation of morality;
but to implant that noble principle
is a work which tranfcends human
ability, we muft therefore have recourfe to motives within our power;
perhaps there are few that have more
influence, than a proper eftimation
of character: both the extreme links
of fociety are fet free by their condition, from the influence of this motive to do well, fo efficacious upon
the middle claffes of mankind;
the elevation of the one raifes them
above the opinion of the world,
whilft the depreffion of the other
finks them below it. Could the female poor be awakened to the fear
of difgrace, by the attention and

N 3   encou-

encouragement of thofe of their own
fex, to whom they look up with
refpect, it might produce fuch an
alteration in their manners, as might
affect thofe of their hufbands, and
gradually accomplifh a general reformation.

Inducements to early marriage,
are the moft powerful agents to reftrain a licentious intercourfe between
the fexes, one of the prevailing vices
among the poor, as the regifter of
every parifh proves, by the number
of unfortunate children, born of parents not united in the matrimonial
bond. As a means of promoting
marriage, it might be worth the
experiment, to beftow a parochial
bounty upon all day labourers, who
marry at a fpecified age, to enable
them to purchafe a few neceffary articles

ticles of furniture, that they might
take poffeffion of their humble dwel-
lings free from incumbrance. The
diminution in the number of natural children, would probably be a
compenfation for the expence of this
liberality.

A profpect of fubfiftence, or at
leaft a poffibility of earning a fuffici-
ency for the fupply of fome com-
forts, as well as that portion of daily
food, which is abfolutely requifite to
the fupport of life, would encourage
the fober and induftrious to look forward to the eftablifhment of a family. The defpair of this attainment deters the labourer from marrying, left he bring a helplefs off-
fpring into the world, for whofe wants
he cannot provide by the utmoft
efforts of his induftry. The confe-

quence

quence of celibacy is moftly a profligate courfe of life, carelefs of the
future, and fatisfied with obtaining a
fupply for the gratification of the
prefent hour; a difpofition inimical
to induftry, and to that perfeverance
in labour, which is neceffary for
amaffing a depofit againft the con-
tingencies of ficknefs and age.

The eftablifhment of fchools for
the education of the infant poor, is
an encouragement to matrimony, and
one of the moft certain means of
producing a reform in the manners
of the lower claffes, if they are regulated upon principles adapted to
this defign; the children, (girls only
are here confidered) fhould be inftructed with plainnefs and fimplicity
in the doctrines of chriftianity, en-
forcing by remarks, within the reach
of

of their capacity, the moral precepts it enjoins, and illustrating them by familiar examples, which come home to their own bosoms, and the circumstances of their lives. The application of time to study, and abstruse theological doctrines, being entirely unsuitable to this great mass of the people, the custom of burthening their memories with verbal rituals, containing dogmas above their comprehension, and unessential to their practice, should be carefully avoided, lest by disgusting them with the shadow, they should be alienated from the substance. The persons who are appointed to the office of mistress in such schools, are seldom capable of instructing the children with clearness on these important subjects, having themselves, but too often,

often, imperfect and confufed ideas
of them: it is therefore defirable,
that infpectors of fuperior information fhould undertake this tafk, at
leaft they fhould fuperintend its execution. The adoption of the facred
writings as a fchool-book, is replete
with difadvantages; the gabbling
manner in which the Bible is generally run over, whilft the reft of the
fcholars are employed in other occupations, deftroys that reverence for
its authority, which ought to be earneftly impreffed. With defign to
enforce attention, let a time be fet
apart for reading it, and inftead of be-
ginning at Genefis, and proceeding
regularly through, it would be much
more beneficial to confine the children chiefly to the New Teftament,
the hiftorical relations of the Penta-
teuch, the books of Pfalms and Pro-
verbs,

verbs, and felected portions of the Pro-
phets, in which are pointed out the
deviations of the Jews, and their con-
fequent punifhment.—The Pfalms,
with a few exceptions, referring to the
particular fituation of David, fhould
not only be read, but may advantageoufly be tranfmitted to memory,
as they exhibit an exemplar of devotion, both with refpect to praife and
penitence. The books provided for
the inftruction and amufement of
charity-fchools, fhould be written
for the purpofe: fhort leffons of
morality, or concerning the inferior
obligations of civil life, in clear language, unembarraffed with difficult
words, and rendered entertaining by
the intereft of fimple narrative, are
beft adapted to convey the knowledge required by the readers for
whom they are defigned.

In

In addition to reading, they ought
to be well inſtructed in plain-work,
knitting, marking, cutting out, and
mending linen, a branch of domeſtic
œconomy with which too many are
unacquainted, who know how to
finiſh a fine ſhirt completely. Waſh-
ing, ironing, and cleaning houſe,
ſhould likewiſe be taught them, with
every other qualification that will
prepare them to become uſeful as
ſervants, or as the wives of labourers. They may be allowed to acquire as much ſkill in writing, as will
enable them to ſet down the articles
of their expenditure, or to write a
receipt, which will be of ſmall advantage, unleſs they alſo learn addition of money. The multiplication
table is ſo applicable, on various occaſions, that a knowledge of that,
and

and the pence table, will profitably
repay the time fpent in learning
them.

The miftreffes of thefe fchools
fhould be recommended to fupport
their authority by firmnefs, tempered
with mildnefs and affection. In
order to difcharge this important
function properly, it fhould be undertaken, not with a view to gain
only, but with a confcientious defire
of promoting the permanent interefts of the pupils. It is of confequence, that a degree of refpectability
fhould be annexed to the character
of thofe, who fuperintend the inftruction of youth, of whatever rank;
for the poverty of the fcholars, cannot derogate from the importance of
that office, which confifts in modelling the minds of human beings,
who

who are candidates for immortality : though the obſcurity of their birth may diminiſh the influence of their virtues upon ſociety. The cane and the rod are baniſhed, by the refinement of modern manners, from female ſeminaries of a ſuperior order, it is earneſtly to be wiſhed, that they were likewiſe excluded from all others, as the uſe of them ſerves rather to indulge the angry paſſions of the teacher, than to produce reformation in the ſcholar ; for where reaſon and kind treatment are ineffectual, blows are never likely to prevail. Severity hardens the heart, and depreſſes a meritorious emulation ; it is generally ſubſtituted for a rational method of correction, which requires addreſs and patience, but by its ſucceſs prevents the occaſion fion of frequent repetition. Rewards beftowed upon the deferving, have a better effect than punifhments, and if diftributed impartially will render them almoft wholly unneceffary.

The univerfality of Sunday Schools, and Schools of Induftry, unlefs deferted by thofe patrons who fo warmly efpoufed them on their firft eftablifhment, are likely to produce a vifible alteration in the manners of the peafantry ; but their full effect can fcarcely be felt, till another generation pafs away, and a new race of parents arife, more civilized than their predeceffors.

Some employments are particularly inimical to the morals of the female poor, among which may be included, field labour.of every kind, where women are obliged to mix indif-

diſcriminately with men of good and
bad character; many of whom have
often no reputation at ſtake in the
neighbourhood, being ſtrangers, who
have travelled from diſtant parts for
the purpoſe of finding work during
a particular ſeaſon. Men and boys
are therefore beſt ſuited to gather in
the produce of the earth, unleſs a
ſcarcity of hands compel the other
ſex to aſſiſt them: when this neceſſity occurs, women ſhould work
in company with their huſbands, and
girls under the watchful eye of their
parents, that they may be protected
from the licentious converſation and
looſe manners of the unprincipled,
who trifle with innocence, and incon-
ſiderately deſtroy the virtue and
peace of thoſe, who unhappily fall
in their way.

Manu-

Manufactories where both fexes are promifcuoufly affembled, and employed together, are perhaps ftill more unfavourable to habits of virtue. Wherever it is practicable, there fhould be feparate apartments allotted to men and women, where each may work without communication with the other. Thofe employments which can be carried on feparately at their own houfes, poffefs advantages far beyond all others; as they promote domeftic affection, and focial comfort; and have a tendency to preferve the youth, efpecially, from the contagion of ill example; whilft they afford opportunities to the mother of the family, to give fome attention to the younger children, and the order of her houfhold affairs.

The

The conftruction of the houfes of
the poor, affects not only their enjoyment, but has a material influence
upon their civilization. The different fexes occupying the fame apart-
ment, is an evil that deftroys that
modefty, and purity of manners,
which conftitutes the beft guard to
female chaftity; this inconvenience
prevails moft in cities and large
towns, where many indigent families are cooped up in one houfe, in
obfcure corners, concealed from the
obfervation of thofe, to whom they
look up with refpect, on account of
their fuperior rank. The health of
body, and purity of mind, of a vaft
number of perfons, are corrupted by
this multitudinous affemblage, whofe
happinefs would be increafed, and
ufefulnefs to the community facili-
tated

tated by divifion; but the daily attention that is now given by thofe,
who are diftinguifhed for eminent
abilities, to the improvement of the
condition of that large portion of
mankind, who are compelled to
manual labour for fupport, will gradually remove thofe obftacles that
have hitherto impeded their progrefs
in morals and civilization.

F I N I S.